(Continued from front flap)

Invaluable advice is also provided women executives themselves on le the ropes in a company, getting the right kind of support, and integrating work and life.

Breaking the Glass Ceiling is a profound book not only for every woman who wants to make it to the top, but also for the men who work with them. It is a snapshot of a moment in a time of change and a blueprint for the next stage of a social revolution.

John J. McKeithan

The Center for Creative Leadership is a nonprofit educational organization founded in 1970 in Greensboro, North Carolina, that focuses on research and training in management. **Ann M. Morrison** (left) is director of the Center's office in San Diego. **Randall P. White, Ph.D.,** (center) is manager of Strategic Management in the Training Division of the Center. **Ellen Van Velsor, Ph.D.,** (right) is a behavioral scientist in the Special Program Division of the Center.

JANIS AND NANCY HAM LIBRARY
ROCHESTER COLLEGE
800 WEST AVON ROAD
ROCHESTER HILLS, MI 48307

Breaking the Glass Ceiling

Jennie —

Continued Success

Best Wishes.

Roy Wh...

5/24/88

Addison-Wesley Publishing Company, Inc.

Reading, Massachusetts • Menlo Park, California
Don Mills, Ontario   Wokingham, England
Amsterdam   Bonn   Sydney   Singapore   Tokyo
Madrid   Bogotá   Santiago   San Juan

HD
6054.4
.U6
M67
1987

Breaking the Glass Ceiling

Can Women Reach the Top of America's Largest Corporations?

Ann M. Morrison

Randall P. White

Ellen Van Velsor

and

The Center for
Creative Leadership

The Management Skills Profile that appears on pages 195–200 is re-printed by permission from Personnel Decisions, Inc., copyright ©
1982 by Personnel Decisions, Inc.

Library of Congress Cataloging-in-Publication Data

Morrison, Ann M.
  Breaking the glass ceiling.

  Includes index.
  1. Women executives—United States.   2. Success in
business—United States.   I. White, Randall P.
II. Van Velsor, Ellen.   III. Title
HD6054.4.U6M67   1987   658.4'09'024042   87-1853
ISBN 0-201-15787-X

Copyright © 1987 by Ann M. Morrison, Randall P. White, Ellen Van
Velsor

All rights reserved. No part of this publication may be reproduced,
stored in a retrieval system, or transmitted, in any form or by any
means, electronic, mechanical, photocopying, recording, or otherwise,
without the prior written permission of the publisher. Printed in the
United States of America. Published simultaneously in Canada.

Cover photo by Marshall Henrichs
Cover design by Copenhaver Cumpston
Text design by Libby Van de Kerkhove
Set in 10-point Palatino by Compset Inc., Beverly, MA

BCDEFGHIJ-DO-8987

Second Printing, July 1987

For the women and men
who participated in
the Executive Women Project

Contents

Acknowledgments viii

CHAPTER 1   **The Ceiling and the Wall: The Double Barrier
to the Top**   1

CHAPTER 2   **Up or Out: How Women Succeed, How They
Derail**   21

CHAPTER 3   **Perception Is Reality: The Narrow Band
of Acceptable Behavior**   47

CHAPTER 4   **Lessons for Success I: It's Not Enough
to Work Hard**   71

CHAPTER 5   **Lessons for Success II: It's Not Enough
to Work Smart**   99

CHAPTER 6   **Breaking the Glass Ceiling: Making It
to General Management**   123

CHAPTER 7   **Hitting the Wall: Facing Limits,
Finding Alternatives**   139

CHAPTER 8   **The Future: Can Women Make It
to the Top?**   155

Appendix 175
Notes 219
Index 225

Acknowledgments

The Center for Creative Leadership made this work possible. David DeVries, the Center's Executive Vice President, and President Walt Ulmer gave us the encouragement and the resources we have needed since 1984. Help came from throughout the Center, and several staff played key roles in the Executive Women Project:

- Mary Michaux, the project coordinator who got us through it without losing her sense of humor
- Sara Britt, our research assistant, who made it easy for us to go back to the data time after time
- Diane Ducat, our colleague who left her job in New York for months at a time and lent her clinical skills to help us interview and analyze the data
- The interviewers who helped us get to more than 100 executives around the country within seven months:

  Ginny Holmes-Lombardo   Cindy McCauley
  Joan Kofodimos   Sharon Sensabaugh
  Vicki Guthrie   Cynthia Anthony
  Jo-Anne Hand

- Martha Bennett, who covered for us in more ways than we could list
- Mike Lombardo and Morgan McCall who gave us advice and support during this project
- Gail Malloy; the library staff of Karen Rickards Hardie, Frank Freeman, and Carol Keck; and others at the Center who offered help at critical times

Many people outside the Center made significant contributions to the project, especially those who agreed to be interviewed and those who arranged the interviews. Others helped in different ways:

- Janet Taylor Spence at the University of Texas, who gave us valuable advice based on decades of her own research

Acknowledgments

- Karen Grabow at Dayton-Hudson, who enthusiastically collaborated at several stages
- Gene Andrews at General Electric, an advocate of the project from the start
- The members of the Women's Professional Forum of Greensboro who were willing "test cases" for our interviews and reviewed our early book draft, including

Jan Blackford	Betty Geraci
B. J. Blocker	Sue Ireland
Daryl Brown	Marie Moyer
Judy Carter	Gloria Thompson
Sue Cole	Barbara Walker

- Julia Kagan of *Working Woman* magazine, and our editors at Addison-Wesley—Robin Manna, Doe Coover, and Ann Dilworth—who helped us put our research ideas into words
- Jay Thompson at Union Carbide and other research sponsors at the Center who urged us to pursue this work
- The many other managers, professionals, and friends who expanded our network, increased our understanding, and added value to this work

The personal support we needed to complete this book came from many people, including those already mentioned. Our special thanks also go to four people who not only gave us the benefit of their knowledge, but also regularly propped us up—Bob Dorn, Mim Clark, Katie McLeod, and Bill Black.

We are grateful to all those who made the Executive Women Project more than a daydream.

Ann Morrison
Randall White
Ellen Van Velsor
December 8, 1986

Doonesbury. Copyright 1985, G. B. Trudeau. Reprinted with permission of Universal Press Syndicate. All rights reserved.

The Ceiling and the Wall
The Double Barrier to the Top

CHAPTER 1

The interviewer was embarrassingly late for the 9:00 A.M. appointment. She had come in the wrong entrance area, and someone had to be summoned by the receptionist to escort her through the huge building. The walk seemed at least two miles long, although the secretary who accompanied her was hospitable and talkative. Finally, the secretary showed her into a modest office, all glass on the inside wall, and introduced her to the head of the corporation's largest division, Ellen Randall (not her real name).

Ellen Randall was a distinguished-looking woman. Her hair had turned from brown to mostly gray, and the interviewer was surprised to learn later that she was forty—she could have been older. She didn't appear bothered by the delay. Instead, she smiled warmly, got the interviewer seated comfortably at the round table at the other end of her office from the desk, arranged for coffee to be brought, and began commenting on the study. She obviously had read the background information and the interview questions sent a couple of weeks earlier. The interview was in full swing within a few minutes.

The first story she told was about an experience that had led to a lasting change in her approach to management. She was about twenty-eight years old when opportunity knocked at her door:

My job change came about when I got a phone call from personnel. They said my name had come out of a computer [as a candidate for a

1

*job opening], but no one knew who I was. They were all curious. This
was the first time I realized that to get ahead, you have to let people
know who you are. I had thought hard work was enough. I started the
interview process, but I wasn't sure I wanted it. My supervisor, a
woman, took me aside after I'd been offered the job. Her boss had
asked me to stay because they needed me in the department; she said,
"I'd take the risk and leave. Don't end up like me, after twenty
years." She pushed me out of the nest. I learned that you have to take
care of yourself. Management won't always help you. You have to
take a risk.*

*My first quantum leap was the move into personnel. Before this, I'd
managed ten professionals; now I was managing one hundred
clericals. My budget responsibilities jumped from $350,000 to $4.5
million. With professionals, you can give some direction and back off.
With a large clerical staff, the issues are different: lots of rumors; a
nonsmoker seated next to a smoker becomes a crisis; getting out early
around holidays is an issue. There was more pressure from customers,
too. They are all around you, and they think they can do your job
better than you.*

*I learned that you have to roll up your sleeves and get interested in
your people. I knew everyone's name and something personal about
each; you've got to manage by walking around. My predecessor didn't
do this. You've also got to dig in and learn the business; you can't
leave it all to your direct subordinates—otherwise you can't help them
solve problems. If your subordinates see you as there for two years to
pick up a management stripe, they'll resent you.*

*While I had responsibility for the training department, I interviewed a
man that I knew was the wrong person. But the job had been open so
long, and I had other irons in the fire. It was over six months before I
admitted it wasn't good. After nearly a year, I told my boss's boss I
had made a hiring mistake. He said, "We had to give you time to see
that and correct it." I learned to never discount your intuition. A bad
decision isn't the end of the world, and relief comes when you correct*

a bad fit. Waiting only makes a situation worse and harder to fix. It won't go away and problems add up. Additional pressure comes from the fact that we had an unhappy staff, and he had a heart attack in the middle of all this. I felt guilty that I gave him the heart attack. I don't want to feel that way ever again. He looked outside the company and got a great job.

She had been in staff jobs with the company for six years, and then she moved into her first line position—another significant event for her:

I didn't know the business. I had to prove my credibility by learning the business. One man there thought he had been the best choice and should have been promoted. I let that go longer than I should have. It was terribly disruptive to everyone in the department by the end. They were just waiting to see what would happen. Having to prove myself to everyone [with that on top of it] was very tough. We finally sat down to talk. We're good friends now. I learned to get things out on the table early. Now that's easier for me to do.

During this period, I went to a convention for the first time. I went with my direct reports, all men. I overpacked. No one had told me about business versus social, and no one offered to help me with my bags. They also did not bother to introduce me to people. The second convention was very different, four or five months later. I'd cleared up things with the male subordinates by then. They introduced me as their boss.

[During a merger and after moving into a line management position] a year ago, I picked up more people and responsibilities. My boss was dishonest and artificial, and gave little direction. There was no cohesiveness among the five people directly under him, except that none of us liked him. The business was being deemphasized and down-scaled. I began to wonder, Do I really need this? Is it worth it all? I know this attitude started to show through. I decided to do something about it. I compared my business to another and realized

3

the other one was entrepreneurial. I put those things into my job objectives and found new niches, new opportunities, new products, and new clients. The job started to have momentum on its own.

I received feedback from two subordinates here. One man said, "You tend not to use your womanhood. You try to neutralize it. For example, you wear a suit instead of a dress." I said I did not want people to use it as a barrier. He felt it could be a tool used in a positive way. Another man asked me, "Why do you sometimes soften things afterward?" I responded that I did not want to be seen as an aggressive female. Maybe I work too hard to neutralize. Now, I sometimes wear a dress, and I don't apologize as much for giving orders.

Her family life wasn't always a picnic, either:

There has been a real strain on our marriage which comes and goes. In a previous job, my salary jumped much higher than my husband's. Then he caught up. When I took my present job, the salary and bonuses put me way above him again. He changed jobs in January after four months of interviewing. He did this without telling me a thing. My husband said one reason was that I did not think enough of the people he had been associating with. I think the real reason is he could become a partner one day and reach parity with me.

Ellen Randall is a very impressive figure. She has worked her way up the ranks to become president of a business unit with full bottom-line responsibility, taken over in tough situations and worked things out, and added executive stripes to her sleeve. She is obviously the one in charge, but she is also warm and open. She makes you think that she's going places, that you'll be reading about her future promotions in the *Wall Street Journal*. She's going to the top, you think.

But Ellen's future doesn't look so bright to her. When she looks ahead, she sees no realistic possibility for further advancement in her corporation. Instead, she senses a wall, a barrier between her—a woman—and a top job in her corporation:

People tell me that I've moved quickly in fifteen years, but I think I would have been in the executive group earlier [if I were a man]. Men with less experience were promoted sooner. After eighteen months in a job, I was told I had to stay longer. They need to test women more. If the boss who hired me for this job had not been there and asked for me, I would have had a lateral transfer once, maybe twice more, before I got to this level.

Ellen sees a limit on how high she can go as an executive woman. Realistically, she said, she will probably have one or two more promotions in her company, but she will probably not reach the top executive level. She is not alone in believing she cannot go as high as she wants. Sharing her outlook are more than two-thirds of the women at or near the general management level in Fortune 100-sized companies that we studied. These are obviously talented executives, and they have worked hard to become successful in their companies. Yet the prognosis for most of them is that they will not progress much farther.

How did these women get as far as they did in corporate America? Why don't executive women move higher? What can be done about the barriers they believe are holding them back? These are the questions we address in this book.

Since the early 1970s, women have made tremendous gains in the business world. More women are in the work force, and women now comprise 33 percent of corporate middle management positions, compared to only 19 percent in 1972, according to government figures. More women also have gotten the entrepreneurial spirit and started up their own small businesses. A report from the IRS showed that there are 2.8 million companies owned by women in this country, and another 1984 report showed that 3.5 million women were self-employed.[1]

It is still rare to find women at the top of America's largest corporations, however. In the Fortune 500 companies, only 1.7 percent of the corporate officers are women, according to a 1986 study by Mary Ann Von Glinow, a professor in the school of business at the University of Southern California.[2] That figure drops even lower, to 1.3 percent, when the companies are narrowed down to only the Fortune 50. Additional figures compiled for a March 1986 special report by the *Wall Street Journal* staff describe the composition of executives in some companies:

- At IBM, the top 6,700 managers include just 500 women.
- At AT&T, only 26 of the top 880 executives are women.
- At GE, only 90 of about 4,000 managers eligible for bonuses in 1985 were women.
- At Chemical Bank, only about 15 percent of the more than 1,000 vice presidents are women.
- At the Bank of America, only 20 percent of the top 3,000 executives are women, even though women comprise 64 percent of the company's officials and managers.[3]

The picture is even bleaker at the very top. In the Fortune 500, Katharine Graham was the only female chief executive officer. Within the past year, a couple more are said to have joined the party, although reports conflict as to who qualifies for this short list. They include Marion Sandler of Golden West Financial Corporation (who *Fortune* noted shares the job with her husband); Liz Claiborne, who grew her own company; and Linda Wachner of Warnaco, who bought her own company.[4] Despite increasing numbers of women in business, women are definitely underrepresented in the most powerful management positions—those in the topmost ranks of the largest corporations that account for the bulk of this country's business wealth.

Newspapers and magazines these days regularly carry stories about women dropping out of the management rat race. "1 in 3 Management Women Drops Out" headlined *USA Today* in its report of a *Fortune* magazine survey of MBAs.[5] Even with a degree from a top business school, women are turning their backs on the corporate executive suite at a disturbing rate. The future for women doesn't get good press, either. Predictions abound that women won't be at the helm of America's largest companies anytime soon.

What's going on? Don't women have what it takes for senior management? Is sexism keeping women away from the top floor? Is it just a matter of time until women in the pipeline break through to the top?

These questions and others prompted the Center for Creative Leadership to sponsor a three-year study of the top female executives in Fortune 100-sized companies. We were getting different messages from various people about the problems of women in management. Some said there was an urgent need to help women succeed in the business world because they are handicapped by their upbringing and education. Some said that helping women only highlights the gender difference, and we ought to let them just fit in as best they can until the increasing number of women eliminates the problem. In other words, why pay special attention to a problem that is only temporary? Some said the world should recognize the unique talents women bring to management and how women can improve business practices. Some said we should just tell senior executives that women really aren't as capable as men, but ask for their indulgence in promoting a woman or two for the sake of appearance.

People expressed some pretty strong opinions at just about every extreme imaginable, but they didn't have much data (if any) to back up what they were saying. In fact, there was little research done on women at executive levels—no way to prove or disprove whatever opinion or suggestion someone made. We pledged to change that sorry state of affairs.

Two of us had just spent a couple of years working on a major research project that identified important characteristics and experiences of executives. With our colleagues Morgan McCall, Mike Lombardo, and others at the Center, prior to beginning the study of executive women, we had interviewed more than one hundred executives about what it takes to learn and grow and succeed in a large corporation. From that study and successive survey studies, we identified key factors, events, and lessons that were important to success. We were beginning

7

to help companies turn our results into tools for use in selecting and developing executives.

The problem with our research was that it didn't include many women, despite our attempts to get them into the study. Only one woman made it into the interview group we analyzed, and only a handful were later surveyed. We were designing tools based on what men said was helpful, or harmful, to men. Do these results apply to women? we asked ourselves. Others asked us, too, and that gave us the impetus to create the Executive Women Project.

If companies are to use tools for executive selection and development, such tools should take into account what is good for women as well as what is good for men. If we are ever to achieve better representation of women in the executive ranks, we had better find out what is valuable and practical for women, what is important for women to develop as managers, what is expected of women in the executive ranks, and so on. If women's experience and growth are the same as men's, human resource teams can have confidence in tools that are designed with men in mind and deliberately use them to help women progress as well. If not, then we must create alternate tools so that women aren't excluded from the channels that help them grow and ascend in corporations. Without research on executive women, the necessary steps would remain unknown.

The Executive Women Project

We started the Executive Women Project with five basic questions:

1. What does it take for women to enter the executive suite?
2. What factors propel women up?
3. What derails women?

4. Are success and derailment factors the same for women and men?
5. Do women need the same opportunities for development as men?

We set about identifying executive women and senior corporate executives who knew successful women in management. Our goal was to match as best we could the group in this study to those in the earlier interview study of male executives so that responses could be compared. We limited the companies we would include to only those as large as the Fortune 100 (in sales and assets), although we expanded beyond the industrial companies to financial, retail, utility, and other companies likely to have women at the levels we wanted. That level was general management or one level below.

It wasn't easy to find the executive women we were seeking. We were fortunate, however, to contact a number of people—professional colleagues and past participants of Center training programs—who helped us identify candidates or connected us with an influential person in a company that had women at high levels. Frequently, prospective candidates turned out to be at lower levels than our criteria allowed. The women who did meet the criteria were often at the highest level ever achieved by a woman in their company's history, and they sometimes had no female colleagues at their level. They were the pioneers on the corporate prairie.

Finally, after successfully contacting twenty-five companies (and quite a few others that could not or would not participate in our study), we interviewed 76 women who met our criteria. We also interviewed another 22 higher-level executives—16 men and 6 women—at ten of those companies to determine the factors that made the 76 women successful. These numbers were close to those in the previous study of male executives, but in that study, we needed to go to only three companies to reach these numbers.

It was tempting for us to discard our stringent criteria and interview women at lower levels or in smaller companies, because we could have traveled less and finished sooner. But the group we identified closely matched the group of men, representing a unique feature of the project—the ability to compare findings for women with findings for men. We will make such comparisons whenever possible throughout the book to point out how women and men are alike or different with regard to attitudes, experiences, growth, and future prospects. And because the executives we studied are highly articulate people, we will explain our results as much as possible in the words they used to tell us their stories.

A Profile of the Executives

The women we interviewed had one thing in common—they held significant positions in their companies that many others, women and men, would give their eyeteeth to have. As pioneers, they became role models for countless others who admire what they have achieved and hope to learn from them. What are these women like?

"The average woman executive is forty-six years old and presently unmarried and without children," according to researcher Marion Wood, the first female professor in USC's business school.[6] Our group of 76 didn't fit this pattern. First, they were younger. The average age was forty-one, and half of them had not yet reached age forty, although they ranged in age from thirty to sixty. Second, only 1 in 4 was unmarried at the time of the interview, and half of them had at least one child.

We were surprised by the large percentage who were married and had children. Seven executives had three or four children, and some had infants. Given the difficulties often cited of balancing career and family life, the number of family women in the group was higher than we—or Marion Wood—would have predicted. However, it was no surprise that the vast majority were white. Only 3 black women were in the group, which fits with other studies showing few blacks in corporate management.

Two-thirds of the executives had already reached the general management level, which means they were responsible for more than one function of their business. The other third of the 76 were poised to move into general management, according to our corporate contacts. They had divisional titles of president, executive and senior vice president, vice president, director, and various others that were tied to such specialties as law or finance. More than half of them were in a staff role at the time of the interview. They ran legal or financial units, or others such as sales and marketing, customer or public relations, and human resources.

More than half of these executives had line experience during their career—that is, they were on the operations side of the business, which typically involves responsibility for profit and loss. The 28 who were currently in a line position sometimes headed an entire business unit. For example, one general manager's business unit had sales of $400 million and assets of $1 billion. The resources at their disposal were varied. Some had huge budgets and hundreds of people in their units; others had only a few subordinates but may have controlled a substantial share of the company's assets. One executive, for example, commented that in her regular duties, a mistake on her part could cost the company millions of dollars *each day*.

These executives worked for a variety of companies, both manufacturing (fifteen of twenty-five) and service (ten of twenty-five). Each company had annual sales of at least $4 billion, up to more than $50 billion. The service companies also met the minimum criteria of $4 billion in sales and $3 billion in assets, but they tended to be somewhat smaller in financial terms and to have fewer employees—about forty thousand was the midpoint for the total number of employees in the service firms versus about eighty thousand in manufacturing.

As individuals, these executives were a diverse lot. Most were impeccably dressed, usually in a tailored suit but sometimes in an expensive-looking dress. Some of these women were short, some a bit plump. Some were unusually tall, with a towering presence. Many appeared to be in good physical condition. Although physical health isn't often a factor considered in studies of executive success, we believe that it should be—the energy has to be there.

In a few cases, the interview came at an awkward time for the executive. One, for example, had just separated from her husband and was visibly upset. She referred to her marriage several times; her responses to our questions clearly indicated that she was struggling with that personal issue. The interviewer commented later that the executive nearly cried a few times. Most of the interviews were part of a long and hectic, but not traumatic, workday for the executives.

As is true of any research, our study is subject to the vagaries of timing and other factors; it is an imperfect study. Our method relies heavily on memory and perception, not simply on facts. Therefore, we can't expect that our data could fulfill all measures of accuracy. And because we guaranteed the confidentiality of the individuals we interviewed and the companies they worked for, we couldn't "check" the stories they gave us. However, accuracy per se is ephemeral in all areas involving people, particularly in management development. Every detail of our results may not hold for every person, yet the patterns found in our analysis, which we report in this book, are solid.

Breaking the Glass Ceiling and Hitting the Wall

We began this research prepared to accept the notion that there might be a glass ceiling, a transparent barrier, that kept women from rising above a certain level in corporations. That's why we retained our criteria for the exceptional women we did interview. In conducting the research, we began to perceive more than one barrier that keeps women out of powerful executive positions. Women who manage to break through the glass ceiling often find that they are walled out of more senior management.

Many women have paid their dues, even a premium, for a chance at a top position, only to find a glass ceiling between them and their goal. The glass ceiling is not simply a barrier for an individual, based on the person's inability to handle a higher-level job. Rather, the glass ceiling applies to women as a group who are kept from advancing higher *because they are women.*

The glass ceiling may exist at different levels in different companies or industries. For the purposes of this book, we have placed it just short of the general manager position. Even in more progressive companies, it is rare to find women at the general management level. The general management level can mean having to deal with the development, manufacture, sales, and marketing of a product. The product can range from a new type of toilet tissue to a new type of credit card. Or a general manager might be in charge of a portfolio of products, each with its specific market and use. General managers in this situation might be responsible for coordinating product development, manufacture, sales, marketing, and overall business strategy for tens or hundreds of products. A position at this level represents a major and difficult transition in responsibility, according to both the female and the male executives we interviewed. In large corporations, these jobs represent less than 1 percent of the entire work force. In a corporation with fifty thousand employees, fewer than five hundred people are at this level.

It is difficult to break through the glass ceiling, but an increasing number of women are doing so. Most of this book is devoted to describing how these women accomplished this feat (or are shortly expected to) and offers advice for others who want to do the same. Once women break this first barrier, however, they unexpectedly encounter another barrier—a wall of tradition and stereotype that separates them from the top executive level. This wall keeps women out of the inner sanctum of senior management, the core of business leaders who wield the greatest power. This barrier has been broken by very few women, and, as explained by one executive interviewed for Hilary Cosell's book *Woman on a Seesaw*, it discourages those who are so near and yet so far:

I think we're being terribly misled about how much success women as a group have achieved and about how real that success actually is. I think there may be a bitter day of reckoning for many of us that's not too far off. A day where women will say, "I gave up my personal life, I destroyed my marriage, I didn't have children, I gave up this and I gave up that and what was it for? I still haven't been able to achieve the way men do, in the same arena they do, the way I was told I could." Let's face it: women are no longer disenfranchised, but we don't have anything like the power of the white male corporate establishment. I don't know if we'll ever acquire that kind of power, but if we do, it's not going to be anytime in the near future.[7]

Chapters 7 and 8 examine the wall and the prospects for women breaking through yet another barrier.

Three Levels of Pressure

All of the female executives we interviewed differed from their male counterparts in one fundamental way. Throughout their careers, they had to operate with three levels of pressure constantly pushing on them. These pressures—of the job itself, of their pioneer role in the job, and of the strain of their family obligations—made their advancement that much harder and that much more remarkable. Let's examine the pressures and how they impact the lives of female executives.

The first kind of pressure that women face is the pressure of the job itself. For women and for men, general management is frequently an overwhelming burden that taxes and frustrates even the most overachieving soul. They frequently face no-win decisions, confront angry customers and disgruntled employees, and make endless phone calls—and they escape home late each night only to feel, often, that they haven't accomplished anything. The demands on executives to handle enormous responsibilities are unrelenting. The work could continue twenty-four hours a day for many executives, so each time they stop to do something else, including sleep, they feel they are falling farther behind.

Executives work at a hectic, frantic pace. They have to obtain vital information in short bursts—brief phone calls or hasty chats in the corridors are not unusual. They are responsible for the strategy and tactics of a business unit, such as deciding which parts of the business to grow and which, if any, need pruning. They must continually grapple with problems that have no "right" answers and often are only symptomatic of some larger, but not yet understood, problem. Meanwhile, they motivate work teams to carry out the business plan, heading forward until new information dictates otherwise.

They must use their extensive contact network—including peers, subordinates, superiors, customers, and interested outsiders—to gather information to guide day--to-day as well as long-range thought and action. And as executives in large, sometimes multinational enterprises, they are on call twenty-four hours a day, since events thousands of miles away may have an immediate and powerful impact on their business. As one executive put it:

For me to be marginally competent, ten hours a day are required, and three to four hours a day on weekends. . . . You gotta love it!

Many things must be accomplished, and the need to do them well constitutes the first level of pressure. Taking new challenges and business risks is built into management, and the higher you go, the more overwhelming the demands. One ad agency chairman who was recently interviewed for the *Wall Street Journal* said: "A chief executive doesn't take time off if he wants to remain chief executive."[8] Achievement-driven people are attracted to executive jobs, thriving on the satisfaction of taking control and moving the organization in the right direction. They typically expect a lot of themselves, sometimes even more than others expect of them. So they endure the pressure to do an enormous job, driving as close to perfection as they can get.

A second level of pressure is that of being a *female* executive. As two senior executives we interviewed said:

There is an element of derailment built into the system for women— the pressure created by having to be a role model and a "first" along with personal competency. Men don't have to deal with this added pressure.

Women are a minority in this business. A woman coming into a high-level meeting will see few other women. They have difficulty finding a supportive ear or shoulder. So they feel distinctly different.

Being a woman where few, if any, women have been before is a liability that creates stress. Harvard professor Rosabeth

Moss Kanter elaborated on the dilemmas and pressures that confront the "token" women at high levels in her landmark 1977 book, *Men and Women of the Corporation*.[9] Female executives are "public creatures" who attract attention with anything they do. They are "stand-ins for all women . . . symbols of how-women-can-do" who must find a way to conform without being self-estranged. In our study, we found that female executives performing in a "glass house" dreaded even the thought that they might fail on the job because it would not only affect their own progress but also limit the opportunities given to the women who come after them. Our article in the October 1986 *Working Woman* magazine describes the pressure to *always* succeed:

"I feel that if I fail, it will be a long time before they hire another woman for the job," one executive confided. Carrying that burden can lead women to play it safe, to be ultraconservative, to opt out if a situation looks chancy.[10]

The pressure is in being a minority, set apart by gender before anything is said or done, and in being responsible for representing women as a group because there is no one, or few others, to share that responsibility. In addition to being scrutinized, a number of executive women are also unwelcome. "There is still the good ole boy feeling in senior management here," remarked a higher-level executive at one of the companies.

The third level of pressure has to do with managing the demands in life outside of work, a dilemma that now dominates what is written about executive women. Women are still expected to take major responsibility for maintaining a household, raising children, even nurturing an intimate relationship. The time demands alone are ominous. But there is also the strain of switching from the role required at the office—tough, no-nonsense, efficient, and so on—to the personal sphere, which includes being tender, undemanding, even playful or sexy.

Their career success can be a stigma for women who want personal relationships with men. "I bet she gives instructions in bed" was one male executive's comment about a woman who performed well in a management role. On ABC-TV's show "After the Sexual Revolution" aired on July 30, 1986, one man interviewed said he would support a woman who wanted to be a corporate CEO. "Whether I'm going to continue to date her or not is another question," he added, insinuating that he would not find such a successful woman acceptable for a personal relationship.[11] The lack of male companions in their personal life troubles some executive women. Others who have a family are baffled by how to surmount the variety of problems they face. The host of issues present in trying to juggle work and personal relationships (let alone time to oneself!) are complex and emotionally draining. The choices and frustrations that face many women who want a "full" life that includes executive status add up to a burden that often exceeds the pressure of the most difficult business decisions. With such pressures on them, it is no wonder that female executives in one 1984 survey ranked self-discipline as the most important quality they had to develop to perform their job.[12]

Two researchers from Wellesley College, Anne Harlan and Carol Weiss, reported in 1981 on a study they had done comparing 25 male and 25 female managers on a variety of factors. They described the "successful male myth," which "assumes that men are highly successful, have well-planned careers, receive excellent training and development, have good working relationships with other company employees, have all their skills utilized in their work setting, and encounter no problems on the road to top management—the position to which all men aspire."[13] This is, of course, a myth. Men as well as women derail, and for many of the same reasons. The same pressures that have such a strong impact on executive women are not foreign to men. It's not a piece of cake for anyone.

Although Harlan and Weiss were impressed with the similar hurdles that men and women confront in management, they also noticed that sex bias creates some different experiences and additional hurdles for women on the job. And the pressure of managing the demands in life outside of work generally affects women far more than men. At higher levels, these pressures can become debilitating. The support systems available to help men are not there for many women. Susan Borman (wife of former astronaut and Eastern Airlines President Frank Borman) says that *no* CEO makes it to the top without a lot of sacrifice from dedicated family members. "Families pay the price. They [CEOs] have had mothers, fathers, wives and children supporting them all the way."[14]

It can be very discouraging to try to manage all the demands and expectations, especially when the standards are high. In *Woman on a Seesaw*, Hilary Cosell remarked:

I am not really sure that it is possible for most of us to fuse the personal and professional into one smooth, charming, comfortable, and competent whole—doing everything our mothers did, and everything our fathers did as well.[15]

We face a critical time for female executives in corporate America. Women have struggled to get into management, and some companies have struggled also to get them there. They have made significant headway in moving up the corporate ladder, only to be stopped dead near the top. At a time when American industry is restructuring itself to face more effective worldwide competition, companies need all of the talent they can get—men and women. We hope our research will help everyone to take a clear-eyed look at the complex problems women face in corporations and point toward some possible solutions. The three levels of pressure that executive women struggle with are not likely to disappear; however, it is possible to ease at least part of the pressure by gaining a richer understanding of what women have accomplished in the past and what they can expect to achieve in the future.

We are at a crossroads in corporate America. Women are stuck below the level of challenge that will satisfy them and fully use the resource they represent to companies. These women, and the executives who want to solve the problem, don't know what to do. They once thought that the increased number of women in middle management would push some into senior management, but that isn't happening; something else is needed if we are to make everyone's investment pay off. People are getting restless, according to Jane Evans, a managing partner of Montgomery Securities, in a June 1986 speech to the New York Financial Women's Association:

Although I thoroughly enjoy the success I have achieved, I am dismayed that so few other women can claim to be making it in the business world. For years, I have felt that it would be my generation that would bring true equality for men and women to the workplace. Contrarily, I find the eighties to be a dangerous and precarious period because corporate and government leaders are beginning to perceive that an investment in the training and leadership development of women is unlikely to yield the same return as an equivalent investment in men.[16]

CHAPTER 2

She started with us at the tender age of twenty-two, with a nontechnical bachelor's degree. In her initial job, a typical female job supervising women, she had peers who were older and had more experience, but she still stood out as having more on the ball. In her first six months, she held three jobs, each with increasing responsibility. Within sixteen months, she held the top job in that unit. She went to data processing for a year, and then she moved into the technical side of the business, a nontraditional area for women. Most of her peers were men with a much more technical background.

She stood out above her peers here as well and was promoted into a third-level management job within five years (not untypical of high-potential managers, or "hi-pos"). After less than a year in personnel, she went into operations in Florida—a promotion into engineering, then two staff marketing jobs where she really impressed the executive vice president. She was rated as outstanding, and her pay reflected that.

The executive vice president sent her into a line job—sales—to see what she could do there. She had no sales experience. She worked for the director of sales in that job, and he taught her a lot. She impressed the executive vice president even more, and he promoted her to a marketing staff job at headquarters. This was a real turning point for her. She had a lot of supporters. She was taken more seriously because of her skills and background—nontraditional jobs, and she had

21

traveled. Three years later, she moved into a line job, and she was picked to go to Harvard's Advanced Management Program.

This woman, now about forty years old, is a corporate superstar, one of the few women to make it into the general management ranks of the nation's largest corporations. How did she do it? According to a high-level executive in her company, a few success factors gave her the edge she needed from the start. One was a high energy level, "intellectual as well as physical—a high capacity for work and detail." Another was good relationships with people:

She always had good people involvement skills. She was aware of the need to make linkages—knowing what needed to be done and who you had to work through to get it done.

Over the course of her career, she got even better:

She's grown in her insights, understanding, and learning ability. She's taken her high energy level and translated it into articulate communications skills. Even when she's dealing with an area she's unfamiliar with, she uses her communication skills for constructive questioning, which is helpful to everyone and makes her stand out. She understands her role as a manager better, and she always keeps an open mind.

Her energy and skills were complemented by other people who taught her and gave her chances to show her stuff and stretch herself—the executive vice president and the director of sales who were her bosses, and one other person in particular. The third supporter was a senior-level manager who brought her into the business and speeded up her job in sales. He has known her throughout her career, and he has moved up even higher in the company.

According to the vice president who told this story about a successful executive in his company, the success factors included both her own capabilities that fit the job demands and the helpful hand of higher-level managers in the corporation. In fact, certain competencies and help from above were cited as key factors in the success stories of the 19 successful women described by our group of senior executives, whom we call "savvy insiders."

Our savvy insiders were highly-placed executives in ten of the corporations where we also interviewed executive women. These senior executives have been involved in decisions about who will be considered to replace key executives (including themselves) and who is actually promoted into general management jobs. The 22 savvy insiders we interviewed included chief executive officers, group and executive vice presidents, and key vice presidents and directors who had an influential voice in these decisions. Some had been with the corporation for several decades and had seen many executives succeed and fail, which gave them a long-term perspective on what it takes to make it into the top echelons of their organization.

We asked these senior executives to describe in great detail two executives they knew personally. The first was a success case, which we defined as a woman who had reached a general management position in their company, perhaps even as high as the top ten positions in the entire corporation, and who was performing well in it. The second was a derailment case—a woman who had been seen as having top management potential and, in fact, had reached a fairly high management level, but who either didn't make it as high as others expected or had made it to a high level but was not successful.

From the detailed stories the savvy insiders told us about these two types of executives, our research team picked out and classified the characteristics and behaviors that appeared to contribute to their success or derailment. Of course, the factors we identified were based on the perceptions of these senior executives. We had no ultimate measure to determine how true they were. We chose to investigate the senior executives' perceptions for two reasons:

- In the previous study of 79 executives (all men except 1), conducted as part of the Center's Research Sponsor Program, this method was used. By asking some of the same questions of people in similar positions, we were able to directly compare their responses about women and men.
- While perceptions may not be the ultimate truth, they are what people use to make decisions. A cartoon recently in *The New Yorker* showed a fortune-teller with her crystal ball giving the bad news to a client: "You are fair, compassionate, and intelligent, but you are *perceived* to be biased, callous, and dumb."[1]

Perceptions are subject to inaccuracy, but they weigh heavily in personnel decisions. Since our savvy insiders made important decisions about the fate of the high-potential women in their companies, their perceptions often became the basis for evaluating the potential of these women.

There were twenty-two success factors for executive women, each of which was mentioned by at least 2 of our savvy insiders. Six success factors are the most important, because each was used to describe at least two-thirds of the successful women. In other words, any successful executive woman was said to have at least a few of the following major success factors:

1. help from above
2. a track record of achievements
3. desire to succeed
4. ability to manage subordinates
5. willingness to take career risks
6. ability to be tough, decisive, and demanding

24

Help from Above

Every single one of the success cases in our study of executive women was said to have had some help from above. This is the *only* point in the entire study on which all of our savvy insiders agreed! The kinds of help they cited ranged from detailed advice to general encouragement to outright testing via visible assignments. One executive wins the award for across-the-board help from one boss. According to a vice president of the company, this executive's mentor had been her boss since 1970. So important is he that "she could easily be a derailment case without her boss and mentor." The boss targeted her in the 1970s to be his heir apparent—he devoted a great deal of time to her, groomed her to be a major manager of the function, and obtained special assignments for her in her area:

The general manager job came as a result of the reorganization. When her boss's job was expanded, he didn't replace himself. He expanded her responsibilities to include running [the area] as one of the subsidiaries. He restructured around her. At the point he turned it over to her, it was her business. She runs it.

Such wide-ranging support from one person over an extended period of time, commonly called "mentoring," was the exception rather than the rule for the executives. In fact, while many executives were seen as receiving some help from one or more bosses, more were said to have gotten important assistance from those higher than their immediate boss, even those at the very top of the corporation. The chairman and a director of one corporation both commented on one executive's good working relationships with superiors, including her previous boss. Both savvy insiders acknowledged that the support she got from top management was important to her career. She had access to the top people, and they encouraged her. "We like her," one said. "We want to help her be successful."

Often, it was a good boss and helpful top executives that added up to a major career advantage. One or the other hired her, taught her to manage a staff, encouraged her to broaden or excel, trusted her, or put her on center stage to perform. They were good role models, advocates, or instructors. As Harvard professor Rosabeth Moss Kanter pointed out in her 1977 book *Men and Women of the Corporation*, sponsors can serve as a source of influence, outward and upward in the organization.[2] One executive's boss's boss worked with her long and hard to ensure that a project she headed was successful. When it was, she got to travel around the country with the company president to publicize the project. She has since been invited to special events as a high-potential executive, gaining more visibility with other top executives.

The good relationships these executives apparently had with the top guns of their company gave them an edge. They had willing sponsors, even tutors in some cases, who had the final say in personal assignments, and they were sometimes included in special projects that gave them insight into how the business works and even more exposure to the corporate elite. These relationships often appeared to be based on personal knowledge of the executive's abilities as a result of working together for at least a brief period, but sometimes the help given was stimulated by impersonal factors:

The effort to pick her up from [one division] was a singular one—we had to find a woman.

The CEO wanted women to succeed.

It seems that these savvy insiders or their colleagues were motivated in part to help certain women move ahead in their company by the Equal Employment Opportunity legislation of the 1970s, to the point where even top executives would challenge and promote a woman without knowing her well, if at all. A few executives candidly explained that a successful woman had been identified early because of EEO and moved speedily through various jobs to finally establish a visible presence as a woman in an important role. Top management supported moving *a woman* along, not necessarily that woman in particular. Nonetheless, their advocacy may have been as helpful as if they had known her personally, because they let it be known in the company that one woman at least was to be given the chance to hold a key position.

Track Record of Achievements

Although having help from above was the only factor that emerged in the description of every successful woman, certain abilities were seen to complement that help and to justify it. A proven track record went with nearly all of the success cases. They "always stood out" in the assignments they took, through their technical competence, professionalism, ability to anticipate and head off problems, leadership, or whatever else the job required. One executive's history was chock full of achievements, some of which boggled the minds of key executives, according to one savvy insider:

She was clearly technically competent. That was very unusual in 1972—we had few women then. She proved she could manage other people. She proved she could handle a heavy work load through others. She didn't try to do it all herself. She proved she could do that and make money for the company. She had eighty to one hundred staff— she could run a smooth operation and sell—she had the balance.

In staff jobs, she showed she could keep users satisfied, plus the staff's attitude was good. She and her staff were agreeable to work with.

When she took on her first executive-level job, and there was no one else from the company to cover for her in the city she was assigned to, there was a dubious attitude among corporate management that she was able to turn around:

We wondered if she could do it. The previous person in that job wasn't very good and probably left some problems behind. Also, did she have "community presence"? Well, she won over the board and the key customers. She showed she could sell and manage customer relationships. And she analyzed her staff—who was good and who was not. She was successful very quickly. The reaction was "We have a well-rounded person here!" Everybody liked her, and she didn't even breathe hard. When she pulled that off, the ball game changed. She became a contender for the executive vice president job. She wasn't before.

The executives who were considered success stories did exceptionally well as producers and managers. One "brought order and control to her department." One had "good work habits—she does her homework; she's always ready. She's much better than the guy who was previously in her job." Another "showed she could run a business." These executives were very, very good, over and over, as the senior executives described them. As one put it, "she delivers; she's able to accomplish things."

Desire to Succeed

The desire to succeed is another factor noted for 16 of the 19 successful executives. They were said to have demonstrated personal drive and determination to succeed by working hard, seizing more responsibility, pushing and persisting until the job was done. "A passion for success" was the way one savvy insider characterized this commitment to achieve.

These executives were "willing to pay the price" and put family life on the back burner, according to several senior executives. Being mobile, never questioning where she was sent, staying single and "not diverted by marriage," and being "much more the achiever than either husband" seem to be indications that these executives were dedicated, ambitious, and serious about their careers. "She chooses her job before her family" was the way one put it, perhaps giving top management the assurances they needed to invest in her development. A 1984 study of 260 businesswomen conducted by researcher Ellen Fagenson at the State University of New York at Binghamton and reported in *USA Today* found that "women at the top are more likely to put their careers ahead of their home and personal life—even though they may have had as many children as women in lower-level positions."[3]

Ability to Manage Subordinates

The ability to manage subordinates was often part of the overall track record attributed to these executives, but it also stands out as an important competency that was said to characterize 74 percent of the successful women. Sometimes their ability to hire the right people was part of the management formula, but more often it was improving the performance of existing employees:

When she was in shop operations, she was able to pull off what others couldn't, such as on-time delivery. She met both quality standards and customer deadlines. She had to manage and work with people who had long service records and highly technical backgrounds. She was able to get them to produce as others had not.

Several savvy insiders commented on the "people involvement skills" these executives exhibited, with open communication and high morale in their groups. When Basia Hellwig, a senior editor of *Working Woman* magazine, reported on interviews with 45 top executive recruiters in 1985, she also concluded that contenders for top jobs demonstrate "strong managerial skills, especially such basics as being an excellent communicator and having strong people skills."[4] For the success cases in our study, earning the trust and respect of subordinates seemed to be a particularly impressive feat when the subordinates were more seasoned and/or men:

She became known as a good manager when everyone working for her was a man.

She ended up as a manager of people she used to report to. One of her managers once told her, "Don't forget how nice I was to you when I end up working for you." He does now.

Dealing with problem employees was another indicator of good managerial skills in a couple of cases. These executives were seen as able to "pull people together to get the job done." They often found the right combination of sensitivity to their people and goal orientation, as one executive was said to achieve:

She developed her own management style. She's very demanding, somewhat unforgiving, but she also looks after her people. They trust her.

Willingness to Take Career Risks

Basia Hellwig, who reported the 1985 findings from interviews with the 45 executive recruiters, also reported the results of interviews conducted by *Working Woman* magazine with 73 rising corporate stars who were suggested by the recruiters. She reported that all of these stars—contenders for top executive posts—"had taken some risk (changed jobs, accepted a high risk assignment, changed functional area, moved from staff to line job, demanded a promotion, started own business) that had helped them to move up more quickly." In 14 of the 19 cases that we know about, successful executives made a job change that was regarded as exceptionally risky by senior executives (if not also by the executive herself!)—a move into an unfamiliar area or business, a huge leap in responsibility, or a transfer into a *lower*-level job that afforded a better shot at the top. Some executives initiated or accepted changes that were said to be unusual for a woman and, thus, hazardous. Moving from staff to line jobs was one example given in several cases:

She has moved counter to where greater opportunity is here in the company. It's harder for a woman in line jobs.

Last year, [one of our field operations] was floundering. The man there was too nice. A young man wanted the job, but he didn't have the right background. Karen's annual performance review came about then. She was in New York, and she wanted to come home to mother—that is, to corporate headquarters. There was one staff job open here, and there was the field job. She debated it, and chose the job [in the field]. I wasn't sure about sending her there, but I acquiesced—she was better than anyone else we had.

The thrust of the transitions made by these executives was to broaden their business experience to include line jobs, finance, human resources, or whatever they could get that was different. Their moves sometimes required relocation or heavy travel, and they usually involved a greater risk of "going down in flames."

Ability to Be Tough, Decisive, and Demanding

Finally, these executives were frequently described as being tough, decisive, and demanding by savvy insiders. "Aggressive" and "strong-willed" were used to describe them, largely because of their approach to business. They spoke their mind, called the shots, and fought for a bigger budget. "She's demanding and hard-nosed," one executive vice president said. "She's never been considered whimsical or wishy-washy." Their tough approach to doing business seemed to be connected to how well they performed. By demanding results of their subordinates, demanding resources from bosses, and taking an unpopular stand with colleagues, they were perhaps more likely to be seen as able to do what needed to be done in the sometimes unfriendly world of business.

The success factors cited by our savvy insiders are similar to what women surveyed in other studies have said about the causes of success. For example, female executives in a 1982 Korn/Ferry survey reported a concern for results, a desire for responsibility, ambition, persistence, and aggressiveness as among the top seven traits enhancing executive success.[5] Similarly, in a 1985 *Working Woman* survey of female executives, more than half of those polled cited hard work, ambition, perseverence, and a need to succeed as factors that got them where they are today.[6]

Other Success Factors

These six characteristics or advantages most often appeared in various combinations in the descriptions of successful executives, along with another five factors that were said to be true of at least half of them. Yes, being smart was one factor, including analytical skills and the ability "to think on her feet." Impressive image was another factor. "She has excellent presence and personal skills. She's confident and worldly," one savvy insider offered. This characteristic clearly encompasses much more than the "dress for success" formula, since the overall image referred to here includes style and stature as well as mannerisms that affect the impression one gives. Sophisticated, businesslike, commanding, and articulate are all part of image, although it may be difficult to separate each component from the total effect. "She made an excellent first impression" is the way one senior executive summed it up. "She stood out by presentation—what she said, and how."

The other three success factors most often mentioned have to do with getting along and getting things done smoothly—working through others, adapting, and being easy to be with. The ability to work through others—down, up, and out—was one strength that includes what many people call "networking"—handling matrix relationships, maintaining good relations with customers, "zeroing in on power people," or "knowing whom to call for what and when." Some savvy insiders called these political skills, some called them interpersonal skills, and one called them leadership skills: "She has a vision . . . shares that with the organization, and gets others committed."

Adapting to the business environment includes the ability to learn "on the run" from others or through their own perceptiveness and sensitivity to the cues around them. "Flexible," "responsive," and "versatile" were used to define this ability, which was sometimes seen as necessary when adjusting to a new or "macho" boss, or when starting a new job in an unfamiliar area.

"Easy to be around" consists of such qualities as gracious, relaxed, natural, and genuine. One executive "didn't act special," another "stayed human, not power-hungry or cocky," and one "says things in a way that's not insulting." Several of these executives were said to have been able to minimize the issue of gender; that is, they apparently reduced the discomfort others had in dealing with a female manager through a "positive attitude" or their demeanor. For example, one savvy insider said, "She's quite feminine, but she doesn't use it or let it get in the way." All of these skills appear to be important for success in the corporate world. Sey Chassler, former editor of *Redbook*, re-

flected on some success criteria in 1986 and included an interesting summary of executive qualifications:

*Management is impressed by and attracted to people below them
whose aspirations are so strong that they do not fear to be themselves,
to say what they feel is important to say because it is what they
believe, to do the job that needs to be done and to act as though they
have a proprietary interest in the job they are doing.*[7]

. . . The Agony of Defeat

There is, of course, also the dark side of success. Some executives derailed on the way to the top of the corporate pyramid,
and our savvy insiders had some ideas about why that happened to them. One executive now in her midthirties started
with her company in the data-processing field and moved up
into field management. She had a technical degree, she moved
along essentially the same career path as some successful executives, and she had the advantage of being a woman at a time
when her division head was told he had better do something
about getting a woman into management. But within four years
of her reaching a fairly high management job, she was forced
out of the company. What went wrong?

*She attained the level she did because she was a woman and the fact
that she had a style that was consistent with the management style of
the division at that time. The guy running the division was autocratic
and she was, too. I still wonder whether that was her basic style. She
misused the power that came with the job. Her method of getting
things done was to go to people and say, "You will do this at a certain
time because the division head needs it. And if you don't, I'll get* him
*to come and tell you." That didn't earn her a whole lot of friends. She
was seen as a pain in the ass.*

Then the division head left, and a new one came who had a much different style. She began working closely with him. There was a question in his mind (and others) about her intelligence. She could give orders, but could she think and understand? He has a very high standard about people he considers high-potential. Her inability was confirmed when she was working with outside consultants on a long-range planning project. She was missing the big picture. They thought she was crazy.

From this point, things got worse. She was working for a vice president who was not all that helpful. He had difficulty dealing with women. He was not a good manager. Her behavior was getting in the way, but he wouldn't tell her. I got the job to tell her. I took her to lunch, and I said, "I can't think of any other way to tell you except that you're a pain in the ass. Change, or you're gone." She heard that but didn't believe it. She had a very difficult time dealing with that— there was a big gap between what she thought and what people thought of her.

I spent time with her. I thought if we could get her attention, we could get her back on track. I tried to explain to her how she affected others. She wouldn't listen. She thought I had another agenda, and she didn't trust me anymore. I finally gave up.

I finally told her the best thing she could do would be to leave and start over. . . . Finally, they eliminated her job. When we tried to place her in another part of the organization, they wouldn't take her. She was still convinced that she was to be the next vice president of the division, and she didn't even have a job.

This executive was ousted from her company after more than five years of service. She ended up not on the streets or on welfare, but in a job reporting to her previous boss, the autocratic guy who once ran the division. One executive told us she had become a vice president at that other company—not exactly the figure of tragedy. She derailed at one company, yet she is succeeding in another. Just as we have narrowly defined what a "successful" executive is (one who has achieved a high management level and performs well in it), we have limited the term "derailed" to the lack of upward progress beyond a fairly high level within one company. (This typically means one or two levels below general management.)

Derailed executives may have been plateaued, demoted, forced into early retirement, or fired. A few derailed themselves, in a sense, by quitting the company when their expectations were not met, even though some might eventually have gone higher. The reasons they derailed, or failed to live up to their perceived potential, at one company may or may not have much to do with how well they are able to do in another organization, if they got that chance. Again, the derailment factors are based on perceptions that must be taken with a grain of salt.

If success factors can be seen as perceived strengths or assets that executives have, then derailment factors are perceived flaws or liabilities. There are three derailment factors, those most often mentioned by our savvy insiders, that represent deadly flaws for female executives. These are most serious because at least one seems to characterize nearly all of the derailers and they seem to be extremely difficult to overcome. They are:

1. the inability to adapt
2. wanting too much (for oneself or for other women)
3. performance problems

The Inability to Adapt

Of all the elements working against her, our autocratic derailer in the earlier example probably suffered most because of her inability to adapt to the new boss's expectations and the culture change that took place in her division. She appeared to isolate herself, even to live in the past rather than face unpleasant realities. Other executives were said to have had similar problems—they couldn't read the environment or didn't get feedback about what they were doing wrong, or they refused to accept constructive criticism and act on it.

Whose fault was it that they didn't adapt? In half of the cases, at least part of the blame was put on these executives' managers for not giving them meaningful feedback for one reason or another:

Men weren't honest and forceful with her. She hasn't gotten feedback.

We did two things wrong: We changed her assignments too frequently. And nobody felt they would supervise her for very long, so no one worked with her. Her flipness and shallowness would have been corrected if someone had worked with her.

In five cases, however, the executive did get critical feedback from someone, if not her boss, and she was said to hold the blame for not correcting her own flaws. When she went through an intensive, professional assessment program, one savvy insider remarked about a derailer, "She denied all the feedback. 'There's nothing wrong with me,' was her stance; 'The rest of the world is all messed up.'"

Inability to adapt was sometimes seen as a gender issue, a situation in which the female executive was at an automatic disadvantage. "She was seen as a 'pushy broad' versus 'an assertive, aggressive young man,'" one vice president concluded. If the fault lay anywhere, it was at least partly in "the system":

To start with, she just never fit into the business culture. She was a pioneer, the most senior woman. She tried too hard to be one of the boys —she rode roughshod over people, tried to act macho, used foul language, and so on.

She was also really concerned with perks, like having a special parking place, her office furniture and office size. She pressed too hard for these things. She didn't have the balance and couldn't read the environment. The result was that no one liked to work for her, and people started ganging up on her.

To compound her problem of personal style, she worked in [a business] which is less tolerant and less supportive than other parts of the company. The system for her was much more suspicious, and management wasn't behind her like it was for [the successful woman]. The work force was older—the "old boy" type—and not as accepting. It was a very judgmental environment.

Wanting Too Much

Wherever the fault lay for the executives who didn't adapt, the problem was their own. This particular executive's problem also encompassed her distasteful desire for the accoutrements of office. Her attitude was similar to that of other derailers who were seen as wanting too much or being too ambitious, the second deadly flaw. "She was a troublemaker" was the way another savvy insider labeled a derailed woman. "She was not a team player. She was interested only in herself. 'Whoever hired her? *I'm* not taking her!' was heard throughout the division."

The requests these derailers made for perks, a bigger salary, or advancement were seen as inappropriate. In a couple of these cases, what they wanted was not more for themselves alone, but rather for the women in the company. "What's the company doing for women?" was the battle cry some senior executives heard, and they saw that as a problem. Making too much of the "woman issue" and wanting other women to get ahead seemed to be as troublesome to the savvy insiders as wanting too much for oneself.

Our research is not the first to point to the danger of appearing overconcerned with equity for women. Rosabeth Moss

Kanter (1977) found that at Indsco (a pseudonym for the company she studied), "one major taboo area involved complaints about the job or requests for promotion. The women were supposed to be grateful for getting as far as they had . . . and thus expected to bury dissatisfaction. . . ."[8] This "taboo" has surfaced in research on black managers as well.[9] On the other hand, Georgia P. Childress argued that it is a myth that women really have it tougher in organizations but agreed that there is real danger for women who accept the myth, rather than concentrate on their networking and performance.[10] Many executive women interviewed in recent years also echoed this perspective.[11] These women may fall prey to being too ambitious themselves, but they are not likely to be accused of lobbying for equality for women.

Performance Problems

The third deadly flaw is not meeting performance expectations. Some derailers fit the classic "Peter Principle" pattern—they were promoted into positions they just didn't have the ability to handle, according to several senior executives. "Not understanding the complexity of the issues and reaching for quick answers" was the problem attributed to one derailer. Other executives' errors in judgment were considered to be performance problems, such as one who failed to keep sensitive personnel information confidential as she was expected to do.

The weak performance described ranged from losing $10 million to less dramatic lowered growth and income to just not doing great. Simply maintaining existing business or doing a perfectly acceptable job but nothing beyond was seen as a problem for some executives, a factor in their derailment. For this reason, the flaw may be interpreted as not only making blunders but, more generally, not being consistently outstanding. That is, it appears that these derailed executives had some failures, but they also came under fire for not maintaining excellence. At least some were not allowed to turn in a satisfactory performance without penalty.

Other Derailment Factors

Other significant derailment factors mentioned frequently were opposites of the success factors, much as the inability to adapt and not continuing an outstanding track record contrasted with some of the career strengths described earlier. Not being able to manage subordinates and having a poor image or poor business relationships were flaws attributed to at least a third of the derailed executives, polar opposites of the frequently mentioned success factors for the successful women. One executive was said to have all three of these flaws, and more. There were indications of her weaknesses, but they became glaringly apparent when she was transferred to another state to manage a newly acquired company:

We sent her there to supervise the young people being shipped in and provide the technical background. She wasn't a leader. There were lots of young people there, but she didn't take the lead; she couldn't impact morale. Instead, she became the biggest whiner of all. She never emerged as a teacher or leader. She just made it worse. Her people wanted transfers. They couldn't get the leadership or counseling they wanted.

She did not have good rapport with customers. She's a giggler—she has a grating giggle that gets in her way. She comes across as a little girl. She loses presence power. She lacked poise with customers.

She couldn't work with others. She's lost her advocates—there's no one there anymore to save her.

She can't hit the high points. She's a perfectionist who gets bogged down. She's not results-oriented—the need for results doesn't keep her moving.

An additional problem for this woman was her inability to be strategic. She didn't focus on the ultimate goal, but instead let herself be distracted by insignificant things. Five other derailers were also chastised for this weakness, which includes not being able to work out a strategic plan. In a nutshell, they were seen as unable to grasp the big picture.

But Remember: No One Is Perfect

It is easy to see how the success factors help executives and how the derailment factors hurt them. It is also easy to slip into thinking that the successful executives had only strengths and the derailers carried only liabilities. That certainly is not so, because our savvy insiders easily came up with flaws for most of the success cases and strengths for all of the derailers.

There were 7 success cases, for example, that had one or more of the three "deadly" flaws mentioned earlier—being unable to adapt, having a performance problem, or being too ambitious. Yet, of these 7, 4 were said to have overcome it and put it behind them, by getting and using constructive feedback about their abilities or their style. That is, these executives corrected a serious flaw by listening to feedback and changing something about themselves, in the opinion of those who knew them. Each of the remaining 3 were acknowledged, by our savvy insiders, to be a somewhat tentative success—that is, the savvy insiders waffled a bit about their future, suggesting they may fall off the track later because of their problems.

On the other hand, the vast majority of the derailers, like the successful executives, were said to have accumulated a string of success experiences that constituted an impressive track record. And most of the derailers were also said to be smart. In fact, one was so smart that "I thought she could see around corners," said one executive. Of the twenty-two success factors, thirteen were attributed to at least 1 derailer. Clearly, the executives who derailed were seen to have some of the same strengths as the successful executives. Yet the derailers lacked three factors—factors that differentiate success from derailment. Two of these—the ability to manage subordinates and taking career risks—never came up for any derailment case, while each was credited to three-fourths of the successful executives. A third difference between success cases and derailers is having help from above—*all* of the successful executives were said to have it, versus only about one-third of the derailers.

The successful executives, then, were not without scabs and warts. What makes this group different from the derailers seems to be their somewhat overwhelming strengths, the relative absence of certain deadly flaws, and the fact that some got the feedback they needed to eliminate major problems before it was too late—whether because they were more willing, more able, or had more opportunity to do so than their colleagues who derailed.

How Do Others Compare?

There is an increasing number of studies being done on female managers and leaders that attempt to get at key success factors or pitfalls. Most of this research has been done with women at lower levels or in smaller firms than those we studied. Also, questionnaires rather than interviews were often used to keep the research cost down, but the responses are consequently more difficult to interpret because of limited opportunities for detailed explanation. This can be a problem in comparing findings from one study to another. We have made some comparisons with other studies only when we felt the method or the results were particularly compatible. As we've pointed out, some factors do seem to be important to the careers of executive women according to the work of others as well as our own.

Another concern with much of the research has been that executive women have been studied in isolation from men. One aspect of our study is that we are able to compare our results to results from a similar study of male executives conducted by the Center.[12]

How, then, do derailed women executives compare to derailed men executives? The results of both studies showed that, as a general rule, the derailment factors are the same for both groups, according to the savvy insiders. Gender didn't determine weaknesses for the most part. Only three differences are important enough to mention. The women were more likely to be cited for a poor image and having too narrow business experience to ascend to the top. Only 1 savvy insider in the earlier study remarked on someone's negative image (he was said to be at a disadvantage because he was short and bald and had bad teeth), while more than one-third of the female executives were said to have an image problem. Also, none of the first group of male executives was said to be too narrow, versus nearly 20 percent of the women. They went up the line of command within their speciality, but without any job rotation, they couldn't go farther. One savvy insider noted that "men tend to have broader experience and, as a result, a better perspective on the business."

Poor relationships with others was the one factor more likely to be associated with derailed men than with derailed women. In fact, every derailed man was said to be guilty of this, but only about one-third of the women. They were described as not liked or respected by their peers and higher-level managers, as having alienated others through intimidation, aloofness, or betrayal. Some believe that men aren't as sensitive or people-oriented as women, which could explain the 62 percent difference between the two groups. Another explanation may be that the women who have made it to a fairly high level have already learned how to balance the ability to keep others friendly while impressing them with their competence, since the fate of women's careers may depend on others' help more than men's do.

This argument gets support from our results in comparing the successful men and women. Although many of the success factors were reported about as often for the men as for the women, there were several significant differences. Successful women were cited more frequently than successful men as

- having had help from above
- being easy to be with
- being able to adapt

Each of these first three factors highlights the importance of getting along with others, in order to be accepted and advance in a male-dominated environment.

The women were also cited more frequently than the men for

- taking career risks
- being tough
- having the desire to succeed
- having an impressive presence

Although most of the success factors cited for women were also used to describe the men in these studies, the pattern of the differences—the fact that nearly all of the differences are higher frequencies for women—suggests that additional criteria for success are applied to women. In other words, it appears that in order to approach the highest levels, women are expected to have more strengths and fewer faults than their male counterparts.

The seven success factors noted more for women than men have greater significance. These are the same themes that came out of the experiences that women executives themselves found to have the most impact on their careers. It is in these areas that the 76 executives we interviewed had learned valuable lessons and made developmental leaps that they regarded as at least beneficial, if not essential, to their success in a large corporation. Their perspective on the basics of success reinforces what the savvy insiders told us about both the similarities and the differences between women and men.

Perception Is Reality
The Narrow Band of Acceptable Behavior

CHAPTER 3

She came into the company in a traditionally female job and was quickly identified as having high potential. She showed us she was very determined—blunt about what she wanted—and very attractive. Stunning is how I'd describe her. Early in her career, she was successful in getting business we didn't have, in a territory which was tough for women. She's always at ease with clients and able to play into their needs.

Later in her career, we sent her to run a new office—a risky assignment—but she was very successful. She recruited a good team and developed her own managerial style. That was when her image changed. She became special.

Over the years she's learned that her success depends on others, and she gets the best from her staff. She's very demanding, but looks after her people and they trust her. She is high in energy, drive, and determination. And she's become comfortable with her success—she doesn't have to prove herself every day. She handles the woman role well. She's positive and well balanced, and is accepted as a role model for other women in the company.

Overall, she has the support and access to top people. We like her and want to help her be successful.

These are high expectations—criteria that go beyond standard bottom-line performance—and they illustrate the success criteria that are used to describe executive women more frequently than executive men. As was the case for the executive described above, women often have to meet the demanding performance standards set for executive men while being seen as outdoing the men in areas where women are traditionally perceived as weak (e.g., commitment, toughness, career risks). To complicate matters, there is an additional attitude with which women must contend—a "vive la différence" attitude that requires women to retain "feminine" characteristics, such as charm and adaptability, while discarding or suppressing those soft or eccentric traits perceived as unsuitable in the executive ranks.

Violating these norms, even in the performance of outstanding service, can be as damaging as poor performance itself. Recognizing and satisfying complex and contradictory expectations is an awesome task, and executive women must accomplish it at center stage before a vast corporate audience. To succeed in the business world, they must find and master the narrow band of acceptable behavior. This narrow band may serve to reduce the uncertainty and perceived risk involved in promoting female managers to higher-level positions. But successful female executives are much like their male counterparts in some basic ways, so concern about their suitability as executives may be exaggerated.

How Executive Women Are Like
Executive Men

Over the years, many people have argued that the abilities and attitudes of male managers are very different from those of female managers. Historically, the perceived differences have been used to keep women out of management. But now it has become fashionable to say that the differences are beneficial, that women will complement men in the management ranks and bring a healthy balance to business. For example, one commonly cited difference is that women are more people-oriented and less authoritarian than men and use a more participative management style. Marilyn Loden, author of the 1985 book *Feminine Leadership, or, How to Succeed in Business without Being One of the Boys*, and others argue that companies should admit women into management because their unique abilities and attitudes will complement those of men, and companies will benefit by having them all.[1]

The basis for claiming differences between executive women and executive men—whether used to exclude or encourage women into these ranks—is suspect at best. Sometimes no data are given to back up such claims—only a few examples and opinions. Any data analysis used to support differences is often based on comparing women and men in general, or those from other occupational groups or at lower management levels. When differences are found in these comparisons, can we conclude anything more than that there are some differences between truck drivers and hairdressers or between company presidents and administrative assistants?

It seems obvious that occupational roles and demands are strongly related to attitudes and abilities, yet few studies that compare women and men in comparable managerial roles have been done. Studies that have been conducted discovered more similarities than differences across sexes, according to a 1986 report by Catalyst. Catalyst, a New York City nonprofit organization, is a respected source of information to corporations on women's advancement in business. A systematic review of research studies that matched the managerial role of women and men led Catalyst to conclude, "Gender differences in managerial style may be mainly in the eye of the beholder." Purported differences in management style weren't borne out in some rigorous research studies. Catalyst cautioned that even the new appreciation for the management tasks that women can supposedly perform more skillfully than men may result in "a new mythology."[2]

Results from the research covered in the Catalyst report, along with other researchers' and our own results, make a compelling argument to support the premise that executive women are more like executive men than they are different in terms of their goals, motives, personalities, and behavior. We compiled data beyond our interviews specifically to test this premise. We searched the data bank of the Center for Creative Leadership for test scores taken from thousands of managers and professionals who have participated in management development programs from 1978 to 1986. We carefully chose test scores only for high-level executives, women and men, of large companies with more than five thousand employees. The tests measure personality dimensions, intelligence, and behavior in problem-solving groups.

Out of the dozens of psychological and behavioral measures, only a few statistically significant sex differences emerged. The score differences suggest the following:

- Executive men are more likely than executive women to feel equal to the demands for time and energy encountered in their daily lives.
- Executive men feel more in tune with their surroundings and are more likely than executive women to perceive things as their peers do.
- Executive men are more comfortable than executive women in an environment where conformity to intellectual authority is desirable and the criteria for excellence are clearly specified (called "achievement via conformance").
- Executive women are more likely than executive men to move in new and original directions.
- Executive women are more likely than executive men to behave as individuals and to personalize their experiences.

These few differences reflect the fact that executive women are pioneers, with few or no female peers, who are seen, and often regard themselves, as outsiders in the corporate environment.

50

These executives are pursuing goals and statuses that violate both business tradition and traditional women's roles. They have few models to go by, so they pursue their goals as individuals, made visible and often saluted by the fact of their differences.

We must remember, however, that the executive women and men did *not* score differently on most of the measures we examined. Our analysis showed that many personality dimensions are much the same, despite some strong opinions to the contrary that have been expressed both in the past and recently:

- The executive women were *not* more impulsive than the men.
- The executive women were *not* better able to reduce interpersonal friction.
- The executive women were *not* more understanding or humanitarian.
- The executive women were *not* more concerned with presentation of self.
- The executive women were *not* more suspicious or touchy.

A few other commonly held beliefs about how executive women and men differ were contradicted by the analysis of personality test scores:

- The executive women were *not* less dominant in leadership situations than the men.
- The executive women were *not* less self-confident or secure.
- The executive women were *not* less able to define and attain goals.
- The executive women were *not* less optimistic about success.
- The executive women were *not* less able to cope with stress.
- The executive women were *not* less outgoing or sociable.
- The executive women were *not* less self-disciplined or rational.

- The executive women were *not* less intellectual or able to apply their intelligence.
- The executive women were *not* less insightful.
- The executive women were *not* less flexible and adaptable.
- The executive women were *not* less even-tempered.

In addition, ratings we analyzed on behavioral exercises that were conducted and scored by professional staff during the programs indicate that executive women are just as able as executive men to lead, influence, and motivate other group members, to analyze problems, and to be task-oriented and verbally effective.

Another recent analysis done at Personnel Decisions, Inc., showed that executive women and men received scores that were much the same on an assortment of management behaviors on the Management Skills Profile, as rated by their subordinates, peers, and boss, as well as by themselves. For example, the executive women and men scored themselves equally on their leadership style/influence, their personal motivation, their adaptability, and their technical knowledge. The women rated themselves higher than the men only on results orientation, informing others, and written communication. The only area in which men rated themselves higher than the women did was on financial/quantitative skills. The colleagues of these executives rated them equally high on *all* the factors measured by the instrument.

These findings corroborate what others found with comparable groups of women and men managers. Anne Harlan and Carol Weiss reported in 1981 that of the numerous measures of psychological needs and motives touted as indicators of managerial success that they used, women and men scored the same on all but one. They measured need for achievement, need for power, self-esteem, motivation to manage, and other factors. The only difference they found was that men scored higher on "achievement via conformance," a difference we found in our analysis also.[3]

Based on evidence from several research studies, then, we can conclude that there are few personality or behavioral differences between executive women and executive men. These facts don't fit with what seems to be happening in the selection and evaluation of executives, however. Despite the fact that female corporate executives appear to be much like their male counterparts in behavior and personality, they are perceived quite differently by many people, including the savvy insiders who can make or break their career in the company. As described in the previous chapter, our savvy insiders listed roughly the same number of derailment factors for women and men in the Center's two studies (4 for women on average, 3.5 for men), but they listed nearly twice as many success factors for women (10.4 on average, versus 5.7 for men). This may add to the evidence that women must perform better than men in today's corporate environment.

Beth Milwid's interviews with thirty young managers and professionals revealed the same phenomenon, reported in the April 1984 *Savvy* magazine:

All of Milwid's subjects felt that, initially, they had not only to prove themselves, but to disprove negative stereotypes about women. They learned: "You're going to have to be maybe not 100 percent better than a man, but 150 percent"; "An average woman is not tolerated. You have to be exceptional."[4]

One executive in a workshop we conducted recently helped create a list of success factors and a list of derailment factors for women. She asked that we not let any male executives see them. Her concern was that they would require *all* of the success factors listed in any woman being considered for an executive job, but at the same time reject a woman who had *any one* of the flaws listed. And perhaps there are some executives who demand perfection in female executives. For example, some men may want to remove any chance of failure before they sponsor or select a woman for the executive ranks; they may feel that their own credibility is on the line, and justifying to their colleagues the choice of a woman for an executive post is tough enough even if she succeeds.

It seems that because women often are expected to be less effective than men in management situations, they must prove that they are *more* effective than men in terms of at least some performance criteria. An imagined sex difference has apparently led to some real differences in performance expectations. The stereotypic views of what women are like also seem to have created some conflicting expectations about how women should behave in the executive suite—*as women*, with "feminine" characteristics, or *as executives*, who are still thought of as having "masculine" traits. Combining the two roles into a coherent set of expected behaviors is confusing and frustrating to businesspeople, including some of the female executives themselves.

As individuals, executive women may be virtually identical to executive men psychologically, intellectually, and emotionally. But the similarity ends there. Women in the executive ranks, or even middle management in most large companies, operate in a male-dominated environment that is often inhospitable. They confront not one set of demanding expectations, but two sets that apply to the dual roles they play as women in business and in society as a whole.

The Hoops

The women described to us as success cases and as derailers were put through a number of hoops as they progressed up the corporate ladder. They had to show their toughness and independence and at the same time count on others. It was essential that they contradict the stereotypes that their male executives and coworkers had about women—they had to be seen as different, "better than women" as a group. But they couldn't go too far, to forfeit all traces of femininity, because that would make them too alien to their superiors and colleagues. In essence, their mission was to do what *wasn't* expected of them, while doing enough of what *was* expected of them as women to gain acceptance. The capacity to combine the two consistently, to stay within a narrow band of acceptable behavior, is the real key to success.

The hoops held out for women in or aspiring to executive jobs were often paired up, requiring seemingly contradictory behaviors at the same time. The trick is to pass through only the overlapping portion of each pair of hoops as they are held side by side:

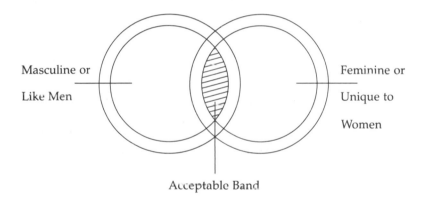

Masculine or Like Men

Feminine or Unique to Women

Acceptable Band

The acceptable area, a narrow band of characteristics and actions, reflects the multiple expectations of corporate women and the challenge they face of blending very disparate qualities. It is clear that much behavioral territory is off-limits to executive women. Women may exhibit only certain behaviors traditionally accepted as "masculine," and only certain behaviors traditionally thought of as "feminine" are permitted, as defined by the narrow band.

The unacceptable area in the hoops comprises the extremes that would make an executive woman too much like traditional, nonprofessional women or too much like women trying too hard to be like men. "Trying to talk and behave like a man can come across as not genuine," one savvy insider said about mistakes some women make.

Some behaviors accepted in men are seen by many as inappropriate in women. Swearing was mentioned several times; telling dirty jokes and smoking cigars also came up in conversations after the interviews were completed. Some behaviors are not so obvious. For example, a senior male executive talked about the dangers of politicking:

The corporate structure can tolerate men who are overly political, but we don't forgive women for this. It's a killer—we associate politics with the gender all of a sudden. There are several women in jeopardy here now because of this.

Certain "male" behaviors are not only allowed, but required. Some savvy insiders wanted to see toughness demonstrated by a woman on an executive track because they believe, as a rule, that women aren't tough enough to handle the job. Sometimes people require the executive woman to *exceed* men on a particular dimension—to be more "masculine" than men in certain ways—to be acceptable. One executive said that the chief executive officer told her, "You're tougher than most of the men around here. Can't you go find some more of you?"

The narrow band of acceptability, then, means that women must be better than men and also better than the stereotyped view of women. It is not enough for an executive woman to ace the success factors described in chapter 2; she must accomplish these feats in precisely the right way, and that means combining seemingly contradictory behaviors.

From our interviews with savvy insiders, we have identified a few of the contradictory sets of expectations for women that must be blended within a narrow band acceptable in corporate life. These pairs of hoops portray the difficulties a number of our 76 executive women said they had, which reflect the pressures that operate on these women. The narrow band for women includes the following requirements:

1. Take risks, but be consistently outstanding.
2. Be tough, but don't be macho.
3. Be ambitious, but don't expect equal treatment.
4. Take responsibility, but follow others' advice.

Finding the acceptable middle ground while still tackling the extremes of each pair was the challenge put to female executives. And meeting this challenge had more impact than anything else on their success.

1. Take risks, but be consistently outstanding.

The senior executives put great value on risk taking, and for good reasons. Risk is the name of the game at the top, with huge sums of money and thousands of jobs on the line, making decisions about whether to invest or divest, compete or retreat, change or grow, all with only a fuzzy feel for the years ahead, when the results of those decisions will become apparent. Taking risks early in one's career is often necessary preparation for top jobs.

A big element of risk taking is changing jobs and taking on new assignments. One savvy insider felt that this was a critical career turning point for highly promotable women: "Taking a job in a different part of the business broadens your experience base and shows risk-taking ability." In fact, many consider accepting any job with a large scope to be a risky move. In 14 of the 19 success cases described by savvy insiders, a risky job change was mentioned specifically. Such risky job changes included tough transitions from academia to industry; deliberate attempts to broaden one's perspective and knowledge by moving into such areas as finance, employee relations, and information services; and the all-important move from a staff position to a line position.

Corporate leaders look for and sanction risk taking in high-potential men as well as in women, according to the savvy insiders in both this study and the previous study of men done at the Center for Creative Leadership. Perhaps risk taking means more to executives when exhibited by a woman than by a man, since women aren't expected to take risks. The stereotypes portray men, not women, as the risk-takers. In fact, some see women's reluctance to take risks as a barrier to their moving up—being "too by the book" and cautious were cited by some of the savvy insiders as weaknesses of women. Women must demonstrate risk-taking to counter that stereotypic view and be deemed acceptable for higher-level jobs.

In effect, *more* risk taking is required of women than men who want breadth of experience in the business. The career moves that the successful women we studied had made—from staff to line positions, moving away from headquarters, and so on—had elements of risk that probably would not have existed to the same extent for men. Moving into line positions, for example, involved not only the challenge of new demands, but also a more hostile, less tolerant environment, according to some of the 76 executive women and even some of the savvy insiders. The risk for a woman sometimes involves giving up a promotion in her staff function, where her presence is less threatening, to enter a new part of the business, perhaps at a lower level, where she may be as welcome as the plague and the possibility of promotion may be slim.

Women are also expected to be extremely competent, often even more competent than men in a number of respects, according to some savvy insiders. The savvy insiders specifically mentioned the outstanding track records of all but 2 of the 19 successful women. These women had been clearly effective in

various arenas, such as starting or turning around a department, handling the media, running a business, managing subordinates and customers, and chairing a task force. One
woman's background included

- chairing a task force comprised of all men, several of whom
  were at higher levels than she, and creating a concept that
  set the trend for the entire industry which got national
  acclaim;
- developing a strategic plan for a male-dominated part of the
  business within a couple of months;
- designing a cross-functional training program for the employees in her department; and
- winning over those who were surprised that a more experienced person wasn't promoted instead of her—"within
  thirty to sixty days, people were saying, 'I think I understand why she got the job [over others here].'"

In general, any candidate for a top job has to be good, but
these women were more than good. Some senior executives acknowledged that *successful women were at least as good as the best
men available* for the job:

*She went through an assessment, and she's a candidate for the top.
She's as good as any male candidate.*

*She had to set her performance apart from the obvious male candidates
for promotions. . . . She has better leadership skills than some of the
men who make it.*

*By the way, she's much better than the guy who was previously in her
job.*

These and other savvy insiders indicated that the women
who are successful in their company had been screened very,
very thoroughly . . . more thoroughly, in fact, than the men as
a whole.

Because of the visibility of the few women in high management ranks, there is little leeway for mistakes, little allowance for weaknesses. These women impressed senior executives with their intelligence and business acumen, their no-nonsense, bottom-line orientation, their strategic perspective, their management prowess, and other talents credited to the success cases that presumably played a part in their track records. Women who do merely an acceptable job, let alone a less-than-average job, may be pulled off the track. Take the case of the young woman who got through four management jobs successfully and then ran into a hitch shortly after the next promotion:

The scope of the management required to do the job had changed. Matrix relationships were now involved, and she didn't know how to deal with people she didn't have direct control over. We sat down with her and tried to work it out, but questions were being raised as to whether she could handle the job. We transferred her to another job in personnel (same level) to get another opinion—that is, was it the specific job or her management skills? Her level of achievement in personnel was satisfactory, but not outstanding. There was no appearance of untapped potential.

We moved her to a job in operations at headquarters, where she's doing a good job and seems happy. But she's not on the executive succession roster anymore. I doubt she'll go any higher than she is now, but I don't think she saw that expectations for her had changed.

Although the risks women take in advancing their careers are sometimes greater than for men, there is no compensation. Performance must always be outstanding, despite the degree of difficulty. If we can liken this to an Olympic diving competition, the analogy would be that the dives performed by women must have a higher degree of difficulty, yet the judges do not follow the customary procedure of factoring the difficulty into the scores they give.

2. Be tough, but don't be macho.

Toughness is another characteristic that savvy insiders said they like to see in executive women; indeed, it was one of the success factors. They praised the willingness of successful women to make decisions, to call the shots in a fast-moving business, and to take a tough stand. These women demanded results from their subordinates, fought for a bigger budget or greater visibility for their unit, or said what they really thought and did what they needed to do to avoid compromising their personal integrity.

Being cool under pressure was another characteristic of successful women noted by savvy insiders that is related to being tough:

She doesn't fall apart when things get tough.

She has great cool under pressure. In fifty corporate meetings, I've only seen her lose her cool two times. Most people would lose it one time out of every five. She's very controlled.

Being tough and cool conveys a "she means business" attitude, which, again, is not typical of the stereotyped traditional woman. Being tougher and not prone to collapse in crises makes these women seem different, which is necessary for them to be considered for high-level jobs. Doing what it takes to show a profit, taking the initiative, and defending one's resources are admirable, even necessary, actions of a high-potential executive. Even such superficial characteristics as being tall—which was said to help give one woman personal dominance and a commanding presence—are sometimes admired because they suggest that these are tough individuals.

While the commonly held fear is that women aren't tough enough to handle big business, the desire for these women to act "like women" still lingers. Toughness, for example, is sometimes qualified or limited to "tough, but not offensive," or "demure, yet tough." And when we look at those who derailed, there is more evidence that being too tough is the kiss of death. One forty-year-old woman with an excellent track record and an MBA was recruited some years ago from outside the company into a job that was a step toward moving her into general management, at a salary of $75,000. Despite her potential, problems developed that made her unacceptable for that critical promotion.

She couldn't adapt to the environment she was in—an "old boy" type of business with older workers who were suspicious and judgmental. She was apparently too willing to be tough—and too good at it. Her macho style and her push for perks made her seem too tough and demanding. Some of her business decisions contributed to this image of her. For example, she got three assignments in a row that took her away from headquarters to assess business units that were not performing up to par. In each case, her conclusion was that the business was a loser and should be closed down. "She got stereotyped. There's 'growth,' 'maintenance,' and 'close it.' She was a 'close it' person—take a lot of people out of work and reduce costs. It didn't increase her popularity."

Being too bottom-line-oriented without regard for the human element, or simply being seen by others as too aggressive, can be as devastating as "not seen as being tough as nails." Giggling or whining, flaws noted in two of the derailed executives, may give an impression of spinelessness or lack of fortitude, but swearing, wisecracking, closing down plants, and other tough acts seem to be equally unacceptable in a woman, even when they might be tolerated in men. Adapting to the authoritarian style of a boss, as one derailed woman was said to have done, could be seen as trying too hard to be one of the boys, yet displaying feminine behaviors could be seen as "cutesy" and ill-suited to the business world.

Somewhere in between is a relatively safe zone to which some successful women apparently confine themselves, where they are obviously female and easy to be with, but also strong-willed and thick-skinned enough to pass muster:

She's quite feminine, but she doesn't use it or let it get in the way.

Her uniqueness is that she doesn't differ at all from men. . . . She plays it just like the men do, and she's very comfortable doing it. It's not put on, not contrived. It's very natural.

3. Be ambitious, but don't expect equal treatment.

According to a number of our savvy insiders and the female executives themselves, many successful women reached the level they did because they wanted what the government mandated. The Equal Employment Opportunity legislation put pressure on corporate executives to find and promote a woman, and the woman they chose in their company often turned out to be one we interviewed. "They needed a woman in senior management" is a phrase we heard time and again from executives as they credited early career opportunities in particular to the pressure put on the company from outside and, consequently, from one or more top executives inside. In most cases, that pressure provided these women with the avenue they needed to fulfill their own drive—the chance to take on challenging assignments, to progress higher in their company, even to experience the satisfaction and the trappings of success within the establishment.

The executives who selected these women to break new ground in compliance with the government's demands no doubt counted on the recruits to want the pioneer role enough that they would do just about anything to take it and keep it. Those who were given an opportunity to fill a high-level position were expected to put the job first, family second (if at all). Their strong desire to succeed was a crucial factor that senior executives looked for in designating high-potential women: "the personal drive and determination to succeed, the willingness to persist and work hard to achieve, and a total commitment to career as the top priority in life."

The willingness to be mobile and to devote themselves to their company, despite the cultural obligations to marry, have children, run a household, and so on, was applauded and noted as a factor in the success of a number of executive women. The burning drive to achieve, to solve tough business problems, and to take on additional responsibilities was heralded as a major asset important in selecting executive women. But their ambition was not so well received when status and benefits were involved; the chance to show their stuff in a nontraditional management role had its price.

According to some we interviewed, being assigned the same responsibilities or the same title as men in the company didn't mean that women received equal treatment in other respects. The salary differential is the most obvious example. Several of the executive women we interviewed said they believed they could be making more money as a man. That may not be true in every case, since one executive woman who had access to salary information admitted that she thought men in comparable jobs made more money until she saw the actual figures and discovered that it wasn't so. But the salary surveys done over the past several years consistently show that women are still paid considerably less than men at their level, even in management jobs and even with a Harvard MBA.[5] So it is not unlikely that these executives actually were paid less. In addition, Harlan and Weiss noted in 1981 that even when the perceived salary differential proves to be nonexistent, a disparity in the budget size still exists: women had smaller budgets than men in similar jobs.[6] Inclusion in the bonus system, access to high-status conferences, and a host of other benefits may also be skewed toward men, as some have claimed.

The women who obtained an executive position often felt that they had to make other concessions, in such areas as pay, perks, and their rate of advancement. As newly appointed members of the executive "club," they felt they were still treated as if they had lower status. In fact, that some women derailed at least partly because they made an issue of inequality or simply asked for more pay or perks corroborates the perception that women were tolerated in the club as junior members with fewer privileges than men. "Wanting too much" was a flaw attributed to half of the derailed women in our study.

What was "too much" in the way of recognition to some senior executives may have been simply "the same as others get" to the women themselves. One woman who complained that she wasn't on the company's high-potential list, even though she had the same background and credentials as those who were, later ended up quitting because of equity issues. Others thought she had pushed too hard.

4. Take responsibility, but follow others' advice.

Accountability for business performance was emphasized repeatedly by savvy insiders as a necessary factor in executive success. One aspect of taking responsibility is making tough decisions, a characteristic admired in successful women. Other aspects include being practical and concentrating on meeting bottom-line goals, and even accepting the duties of a supervisory role. These also emerged as success factors.

Taking responsibility for business operations is a critical part of building a track record. Another responsibility executives have is their own career, a lesson learned by a number of women as they advanced—it is up to the individual herself to keep her career moving, to get breadth of experience and exposure to the right people, to get into mainstream positions, to get credit for her accomplishments, and so on. Savvy insiders generally agreed that more senior executives, sometimes including themselves, may offer help and nudge women along, but they do not accept responsibility for someone else's career.

Senior executives expect women to decide what they want and go for it. On the other hand, if their decisions and wants don't match what senior executives want *for them,* problems often result. Senior executives sometimes seem to expect women to accept whatever advice and opportunities they offer, to do as they are told regarding career moves. For example, proposing an alternative to a promotion offered or trying to negotiate the terms instead of automatically accepting it was considered an affront by some senior executives.

One woman was admired because she wasn't intimidated by executives. "She called things as she saw them" and, because of her good judgment, she was offered a management job that was considered to be a stepping-stone to general management, but not without risk. Previously, another woman had turned the job down. So this woman tried to bargain, asking senior managers what the job would do for her and what they would do for her if she accepted. When she got nowhere on this tack with management, she turned the promotion down, and that didn't please top management. Her progress in the company subsequently slowed down.

Some senior executives regarded taking advice and criticism as a strong, positive factor in the struggle of women to adapt to the workplace. Listening to feedback was a success factor cited for 7 of the 19 successful women described by savvy insiders:

She had a tendency to get visibly upset if something was happening that she didn't like, and also to be very defensive. I spoke to her about the first problem, and she changed. One of her great assets is the ability to listen and make changes.

Responding to this feedback was probably a good decision by the woman. It seems to be a clear example of when a woman should trust someone who is in the know and has her interests at heart. Not all of the advice that female executives encounter is that clear, however. Several of our female executives said that it is important to trust people, but only certain people. Some also said they came to understand that others' motives are not the same as your own—when others offer help, it may or may not be to your advantage to accept it, or even to believe they are being helpful. This caveat applied to promotions and job transfers that were offered, and it also applied to more general advice they received about their behavior.

One savvy insider identified the "greatest weakness of people" as "being unable to trust others, to put your career in their hands." Although the assistance that women received from senior executives in getting new opportunities was vital to their career, these women also realized that they had to choose what was best for themselves and not always depend on others to know what that was. They often had to rock the boat, to turn down high-level staff positions for lower-level line positions, to make an issue of being put into a replacement chart or getting tuition reimbursement to attend an executive program, in order to get what they believed they needed for their career enhancement instead of what was offered to them. Some said they realized that senior management wanted a woman in a certain job only because of public appearance, not because it would be a good fit with their talents or goals. Sometimes pushing too hard or going against the wishes of top management helped derail them, even when they had logic on their side.

Women executives have a tough time deciding from whom to get advice and how appropriate the advice is for them. That the willingness to listen to feedback is a success factor mentioned only by those savvy insiders who were men is interesting. Perhaps more senior men feel a greater need than women to counsel up-and-coming female executives. Or perhaps men see the willingness of women to make changes based on their advice as an indication of women's accepting junior status in the executive club, which may make them easier to be around. Whatever the case, women are left with the tough decisions about what advice to solicit, from whom, and what to do about the advice they obtain.

The Hoopla

The hoops that executive women confront are not for the faint-hearted. They represent tough battles to be waged throughout a career, battles that get a great deal of corporate attention. The women who are willing to face the hoops, and especially those who successfully maneuver their way through the narrow band within the hoops, are thoroughly scrutinized by senior management, male peers, women at lower levels, their relatives, headhunters, the media, and so on. Much hoopla surrounds their tests and their achievements.

Of course, men are also tested. The demands on men who choose to pursue the executive ranks is no "Life of Riley." Men succeed and derail for many of the same reasons women do, according to the factors identified by savvy insiders. The men who derail surely suffer as much anguish as women. There are even some groups of men who experience some of the same biases and pressures as women. Hurdles that keep minority managers out of top jobs, according to the *Wall Street Journal* and other sources, are not unlike those that women face—having to work harder and longer than white men to get the same things, being sidetracked into staff jobs, isolation, and so on.[7]

Another group of men who face bias and resentment are the sons and other relatives of company leaders who are on the management team, from small family businesses to large corporations. These men are also isolated; very visible, they are often the target of other workers' hostility, and their abilities are considered suspect. Their colleagues are often tempted to believe that these men were hired and stay only because they are family, and not because they are good. Colleagues of female executives sometimes believe that these women have management positions only because of pressure to meet EEO guidelines.

Although some special groups of men encounter hurdles similar to those of women in management, the hurdles for women seem to be more numerous and bigger because of the three pressures we described in chapter 1 that are always operating on them. The demands of the job itself are tough on anyone, and they may be tougher for minority men and male family business managers than for other men, as they apparently are for many executive women. Minority men also experience the bias that comes from centuries of stereotyping, as do executive women. Men typically do not have responsibility for home and family care, however, so they have some relief from the time, worry, and conflicting expectations that are part of such pressure. One black executive interviewed for the *Wall Street Journal* told the reporter, "I always tell young blacks you need a very good wife who can support you."[8] It is clear to us that the hoops executive women must maneuver today are more difficult than those confronted by men.

Women experience the special hoops and the hoopla that they do in management because executive women and men have been perceived as more different from each other than they really are. Mounting evidence indicates that, when careers are matched, women are remarkably similar to men in their characteristics, abilities, and motives. Yet the enormous and sometimes contradictory expectations that people have of women are the result of sex role stereotypes that continue to pervade the thinking of otherwise rational individuals. Stereotype-driven perceptions have led to unrealistic expectations of executive women, and these expectations are part of the environment in which the women must work and live. This environment is qualitatively different from the environment executive men operate in, and this difference may be the crucial—and the only meaningful—difference between male and female executives.

That the most important difference may be externally based and not intrinsic is little comfort to the women who face stiffer criteria than men and very discouraging odds for success in the executive suite. The women we interviewed are the success stories in environments where, as one put it, "perception is reality." Yet we found that the lessons most crucial to their success are much the same as the lessons reported by male executives. Of the fifteen most frequently mentioned lessons that women and men said resulted from their key experiences, the majority are essentially the same. In other words, the same things need to be learned by anyone. But the opportunities to learn these lessons are not the same for women and men because the environment is different. How these successful women navigated their way through the narrow band within the hoops and the hoopla—to gain the experiences and to learn the lessons important to succeeding as a manager—is the substance of their stories.

Lessons for Success I
It's Not Enough to Work Hard

CHAPTER 4

She welcomed the interviewer into her cluttered office a little after 10:00 A.M. There were stacks of papers on her desk and on the floor near the desk, so the interview was conducted at the adjacent round table. She already had read the interview questions and was prepared to talk about herself.

In two and a half hours, she portrayed corporate life from her vantage point—a thirty-six-year-old woman who has a husband and two children, goes to church, is active in the community, and in fifteen years with her company, has worked up to general management of a line function. Her stories covered three jobs, starting with one she held at about age twenty-three:

My first managerial job was an "acting" position, a three- to four-month assignment for which there was no precedent. It was a trial. They picked three women, all young like me, and we wrote methods and procedures. We expected we'd hand them over, but once that part was done, we were each assigned to head up a part of the operation, to implement the methods for another three months over the summer.

I supervised three hundred people, in clerical jobs. I recruited college kids for the summer; I had to fire someone for the first time; there were braless women, drug use, and so on. I had to wing it. I didn't see light that summer.

My boss for the first three months was wonderful. She was an old-school nurturing type who had made it to first-level supervisor after

*years and years with the company. She taught me how to accept
criticism. I also learned to get comfortable with uncertainty. To face a
challenge, you give it your best shot. You have to trust your instincts.
And I really learned how to manage people—to be unafraid of
confrontation, unafraid to praise. I learned who to trust.*

*[About a year later] I was challenged to take a nontraditional job in
engineering. A manager two levels higher said I couldn't do it. A
woman is too feminine, he said; people wouldn't take me seriously. He
told my prospective boss in the engineering department, in front of
me, "I think you're taking a big chance with this one, but it's up to
you."*

*That forced me to take stock. Do I prove him wrong? Do I stay with
the company? I took the job. I wasn't confident, but the challenge was
exciting. I decided that the manager wasn't malicious; he was just
attempting to counsel me—"Let me tell you, little girl." I believed my
competence would show. It was the first time I encountered
discrimination. I wasn't wanted. People felt I had no right to be there.
It was a live-or-die situation.*

*My first project in that job was to solve a technical problem. I had to
get people to teach me without resenting me. One male peer gave me
to one of his subordinates—"He'll help you," he said. He wouldn't
even talk to me once he discovered I was a woman. I learned how to
present myself in a nonthreatening way without compromising my
sense of self.*

*A frightening first for me was when my boss told me I had to put in
my time in the field. I went into a marketing role at an affiliate
company. I had no background in marketing. I didn't understand the
affiliate's structure, and I didn't know anyone there who could help
me. I couldn't even read the company's phone directory!*

*I took a cut in pay. I was very frightened by the challenge, and I
wasn't sure I could get back. I had to trust my boss. I spent a year
there, and it was the worst year of my life. People didn't understand*

why I was there. They thought it was a promotion for me, that I took the job from someone there. I was the only woman in the department. No one helped me. And there were malicious things done to me in the first few weeks. They took the casters off my chair and rigged my desk drawer.

I cried a lot for a year, walking from the train the three blocks to my house. During the day, I learned and did what I was supposed to do. I went outside my group to learn what I could. I never admitted that they were getting to me. I was determined to get out successfully, and I did. I was offered a promotion out of there.

[Another career move was] a quantum leap, level-wise. It was the first time I felt I might not be able to handle the job. Others at that level had experience, and I respected them. I had to catch up. I was afraid I wouldn't be accepted. I was so young, plus I was the first woman at that level. Youth in a woman is more troublesome than in a man.

One of my first assignments in that job was to write speeches for my bosses to present to legislative bodies, in addition to my regular job. I worked until ten at night. I learned they were people like me, with the same fears—competence, acceptance, whom to trust. I went from seeing them as demigods and superheroes when I was down in the ranks to starting to see them as more experienced people like me. I called them if I wanted help, and I called them to clarify their requests. I didn't use memos. I learned to cut through the bureaucracy and save time.

These and other experiences this executive had led her to advise that younger managers not chart too narrow a career:

You need to be willing to diversify. Take challenges that will round you. Take anything that will help you understand how the business works. Most of my moves have not been deliberate. I'm well rounded now. I can go lots of places next. Knowledge is an important component of success, especially for a woman.

The interviewer was impressed by her and by what she said. The executive was distinctively dressed—her suit had a pleated collar—not a run-of-the-mill outfit, yet not at all fluffy, and a contrast to the messy office. She was open about her experience and her feelings. The entire interview had been done with her office door *open*, and her secretary sat just outside the door. She was friendly and solicitous. She walked the interviewer back out to the street to be sure transportation was available. And she was successful, with career options at her fingertips. She had stated:

There's no formula for success. The total package needs to be right. It's not just intelligence. The package includes integrity, judgment about when to fight, and being someone senior managers can picture in the boardroom. Some gifts are given, not made. You can't always learn these things.

This executive and the other 75 women we interviewed about their own experiences had many stories to tell and some strong feelings about what it takes for a woman to succeed in business at their level. And what they said they had learned is closely related to the pressures and the hoops that they confronted in their quest for corporate stardom. The lessons represent developmental leaps that they made to cope with the demands placed on them. There are six developmental leaps that pervade the experience and advice of these 76 executives to such a great extent that we believe they are requirements for success—what female executives must do to succeed in a large corporation.

The six lessons for success are as follows:

1. Learn the ropes.
2. Take control of your career.
3. Build confidence.
4. Rely on others.
5. Go for "the bottom line."
6. Integrate life and work.

These lessons can't be isolated from one another, because, as the executive quoted above expressed it, "the total package needs to be right." These lessons are much like the success factors reported by our savvy insiders—it is the balance among them that counts most heavily, yet each one is important in itself.

It is probably true that not everything needed for success can be learned, but plenty *can* be learned and some lessons *must* be learned. It takes more than hard work to be successful, our executives discovered. Learning the ropes, directing their career, and being confident in themselves were also needed. This chapter explains these first three lessons; the next chapter covers the final three lessons for success.

Lesson 1: Learn the Ropes

It doesn't matter how good you are. You have to understand the rules, if only to find out how to survive.

She didn't understand the culture, or she didn't know how to get things done, or she was oblivious to what people were saying about her, or she insisted on being different from everyone else. These are some of the reasons given when an executive derails. Executive careers often are stopped because of undocumentable, even unexplainable, factors. "She just never fit in," the executives murmur to themselves as another high-potential executive disappears.

A revelation for some executives in our study was that doing a good job—being smart and working hard—wasn't enough to propel them up or keep them from derailing. They came to understand the importance of fitting in. "Believe me," a retired CEO advised us recently at an informal gathering, "what can be put on paper doesn't make the difference in selecting high-level executives."

Women begin with a disadvantage, since they are an unknown commodity on mahogany row and are clearly different in some respects. The "chemistry" is much less certain, and therefore, the risk is greater. Those who succeed find ways to be similar, to minimize differences, to become more familiar, predictable, safe. They identify what constitutes the narrow band of acceptable behavior in their company, and then they adjust their actions and attitudes to fit. In short, they learn the ropes.

Learning the ropes is a way to gain acceptance. It involves getting acquainted with the system and doing what those in power will like, respect, and reward (or at least accept). Every manager does this to some extent. The successful executives we studied were adept at learning the ropes, and they did it in two ways: they did much observing, and they actively solicited feedback on their own performance and on company expectations in general. Interacting with senior executives in their companies turned out to be the key to identifying what was expected of them:

As a lawyer in the company, I was exposed to upper-level executives, including the chief executive officer. I was expected to advise them and participate in the decision making. I learned that the packaging and style of both you and your ideas are important. You have to be able to present things in a nonthreatening fashion. You yourself have to be nonthreatening. You have to understand the "rules of the game" and what's expected of you. For example, I heard several executives talking about a white male who wasn't going to go anywhere because he wore white socks to work his first day.

One manager was privy to a high-level meeting in which marketing decisions were made. What she learned by watching these executives in action shaped her own self-improvement plan:

It opens your eyes. People sit in a room and use their best judgment. There are no right or wrong answers. Higher levels don't necessarily make right decisions, but a decision is made. The smartest person is not the one to succeed. Success is measured more in terms of ability to influence.

She began to develop the skills that would make her more convincing instead of trying only to be smarter. Other executives also had experiences that led them to focus on skills that would foster visibility, credibility, and credit for the work they did. This developmental tack is similar to the route many successful male executives choose to take. We learned from our study of men that intelligence without these other capabilities can be a deadly flaw. One can be considered by others to be *too* smart! And this liability may be especially true for women. Brilliance can make them intimidating, which may be more threatening in a woman than in a man.

Learning by observing other people wasn't always a positive or even a neutral experience. The executives we interviewed learned much about the system from seeing the dolts, dullards, and downright nasty people who were promoted to positions above them—sometimes as their direct supervisor. Being assigned such a bad boss, or simply noticing that individuals with negative qualities can go very high in the corporation, was a shock for many executives, one that sometimes led to a bit of cynicism and some self-protection.

Another rich source of lessons about what is necessary for success in an environment is what other people tell you. Helpful bosses and advocates were often full of advice for our executives about how to get the attention and recognition they needed to move up. Often, they were able to recommend the key positions to attract the right kind of attention. More important, they offered feedback on how an executive might better conform to the expectations of the organization.

Many of the women we interviewed made it a point to solicit feedback from more senior men in the company. One even scheduled an appointment each year with the president, several levels above her, to hear his assessment of her progress and potential.

Since popular opinion holds that corporate rules are passed in informal conversation more than any other way, getting the inside scoop from peers is essential to learning the ropes. But women are left out of those conversations, according to many women and men. Some female executives have gone to great lengths to be included in the network after a while—they learned sports, did favors for peers, or backed down on an issue, for example. Even so, the circle remained closed to some, and they had to get along without that network or be more creative about getting information from it. One executive took an indirect approach, with the help of a friend:

I was excluded from an "old boy" network, but I found a way in. A male peer and I were new in the business. The business had an "old boy" network that was crucial to knowing what was going on. I was excluded because I'm female, and my male peer was excluded because he was new. We became friends and supported each other. Gradually, the network started to include my friend, and he would keep me informed of what was going on. Pretty soon he told me that he couldn't be too closely associated with me (such as going out to lunch or being seen talking) or the network would stop considering him as "one of the boys." I accepted this (I didn't want to hurt his career), so we started doing most of our talking on the phone after work. Thanks to my friendship with this male peer, I know everything that goes on. He's my "in" to information I otherwise wouldn't be able to access.

What did our executives learn from observation and feedback? Although the specifics varied from company to company, there were five general elements that described the narrow band of acceptable behavior.

1. *Women executives are expected to be nonthreatening.* "She's quite feminine, but she doesn't use it or let it get in the way" and "She handles the woman role positively; she's well balanced" are comments that suggest women have a weapon that men don't have but don't feel they have to resort to using it to be successful. Women trying to hide their femaleness by acting like men, and women making their femininity a factor to be reckoned with, are the extremes to be avoided. Often the woman has to figure out what that means, because top management knows it only when they see it. "Being too feminine" is a fatal flaw for women, according to one male executive. When pressed to continue, he could only say, "It's hard to explain."

Many in our group of successful women were noticed and used their visibility to advantage. One executive understood that she was a curiosity to top management because of her unique role in the company. She made appointments with executives who would not be accessible to any man at her level, knowing that they would see her out of curiosity. Another executive said she was allowed more time in meetings with key executives than are men. She had more time to state her case and field objections because executive men wanted to see what she would do (and perhaps also because the gentlemen found it more difficult to kick a lady out of a meeting).

Some women adapted by being deliberately nonconfrontational with executive men "to get them to feel comfortable." Women who developed clever ways to avoid petty arguments found that their effort impressed their superiors and helped them fit in:

People didn't ask me to lunch because it wasn't considered proper for a woman to pay for her own lunch. There was always an argument about who would pick up the check. I have had clients who would try to buy me lunch. Now when I have to take someone out, I take them to clubs where I'm a member.

2. *To be taken seriously, women need to do well in a position that has credibility in their company.* The credible jobs are often those in

79

operations, management jobs with profit-and-loss responsibility, or key roles in sales and marketing. These are often the same jobs that are used "to separate the men from the boys," according to our savvy insiders. The logic seems to be that if a woman wants to contend for top jobs along with the men, then she has to prove her ability in jobs that are critical to the company, just as any serious male candidate must do. The jobs seen as most central or most difficult differ from company to company, even within the same industry. Therefore, the challenge is not only to perform well, but also to identify and obtain key jobs.

3. *The executive women needed to succeed at managing certain people, men and minorities in particular.* It is difficult enough to hire, train, and motivate people in general—this was cited as a success factor for men as well as women in our studies. But where the rubber meets the road for women trying to be accepted is in successfully supervising men and in dealing with minorities. If men will work for a woman, particularly men with seniority or those who once were her peers, then she must be good, the premise seems to be.

Dealing with troublesome minorities or women is another aspect of supervision that seems to be a test for women. The female executives who had to discipline or fire another woman or a black subordinate found it extremely painful, and this was the most frequently reported act of procrastination, as confronting any problem employee had been for the men previously interviewed. They fear making a mistake or not doing enough as a manager and, as a consequence, hurting someone. They may also realize that these people have been handicapped as minorities in the corporate world and not want to deny them a break. This situation seems to be a test of whose side the woman is on and where her loyalties lie.

The women who went through such an ordeal spoke of their need to be fair to the employee and yet also accept only competent people on their staff. They could not afford to keep someone who couldn't carry a big share of the work load or who would hurt morale. With the many expectations others had of them as managers, they needed a team that could deliver. This test may be the most revealing to and about women struggling to reach the top. It is part of "the bottom line."

4. *They learned to trust their superiors.* One savvy insider said it bluntly in describing some fatal flaws: "Being unable to trust others, to put your career in their hands—this is the greatest weakness of people, both women and men." Some top managers want young candidates to put their fate in their hands. They may feel the need to be in control, to be the guru dispensing knowledge, gatekeepers of the top floor. They want to be asked for permission and for counseling, so that it is clear who is in charge. Our savvy insiders seem to value the role of giving advice, since listening to feedback was a success factor.

It seems that women are expected more to seek counsel from their superiors than are men. Seven of our 16 male savvy insiders mentioned listening to feedback as a success factor, but none of the 6 female savvy insiders did. And the feedback they described involved admitting mistakes and acknowledging weak spots. The message seems to be that if top managers are willing to risk telling a woman what's wrong with her, then she had better accept it and do something to improve.

5. *Don't expect too much.* When describing the biggest challenge they ever faced, 6 executives said that it was simply being a female executive. The responsibilities thrust upon them included accepting the limits imposed on them. As women, they realized that they would be permitted to fit in only in certain respects, only as it would benefit the company and those in charge of it.

Some of our executives pushed those limits, and some took what was offered, knowing that to expect to be more than an unwanted, junior member of the club would be unreasonable. That they were willing to accept less than they deserved was significant. They felt this was necessary if they were to fit in at all. One executive's boss was promoted to head the department, and a replacement for her boss was sought outside. She was not considered seriously for the promotion until the initial search proved unsuccessful. Eventually she did get the job, for three reasons:

1. The president of the company knew who she was, since he had been impressed by a position statement she had prepared for him earlier on an issue important to the business.
2. Higher management didn't want to discourage the young men who worked for her. It was important to show them that the company promotes from within so they would stay motivated.
3. "I was cheap."

Despite her ability and experience, she believes that without these other reasons, she wouldn't have received the promotion. And reinforcing reason number three, other female executives said they would be paid more if they were a man. One savvy insider corroborated:

Women work harder and for less money. Women will accept pay cuts for development. This is an advantage because senior management wants the best for the least price.

Because of the "value" women represent, those who want equal rewards for their contribution may be seen by others as wanting too much. Women are much more acceptable when they cost less—without that factor, the incentive to include them may be eroded.

We believe that the successful women usually are those who have a good sense of how much investment, in money and time, they can demand, and they accept that. They do what they can do.

One of the success cases described by our savvy insiders also was interviewed directly as a part of the group of 76. She was said to have a number of success factors on her side, including several that indicate she had learned the ropes quite well: she has an impressive image, she is able to work through others, she is cool under pressure and easy to be with. "She's approachable yet clearly in charge. She's not intimidating," said one senior executive. "She's stayed human. She's not power-hungry. She's confident in a positive way, not cocky." As the savvy insiders told it, her good relations with customers stood out when she took over a new region for the company. She charmed the board as well as key customers and everyone else, and she impressed senior management with her ability to handle a heavy work load by delegating effectively rather than trying to do it all herself. And when she encountered a boss who was close to intolerable, she trusted the advice that she sought from these same executives.

These characteristics and behaviors endeared her to top management. The regional job and the bad boss were tests for her, and she aced them both. But she came close to failing them. As she tells these stories, success nearly slipped through her fingers, but two events saved her. First, a couple of years before taking the regional job, someone told her that she *was* intimidating. "I was people-oriented with my customers but not with my subordinates," as she described it. Getting that feedback was key for her, because she realized that her perception of herself and her own style was not the same as what others saw, particularly her people. She resolved to spend more time with her subordinates than she had previously.

A couple of years after she received that feedback, she changed jobs and worked under a boss she couldn't stand. "I threatened him big-time," she said, because of her longer experience in the area and faster movement in the company. In contrast to her style, her boss was authoritarian and political. And he resented her, probably because he attributed much of her success to being a woman. She put up with him for a full year, having requested a move to no avail, and then decided to leave the company.

When a top executive learned about her decision, he talked her out of it and promised her a promotion. She explained to us that she sat there for a year because she hadn't let senior management know how strongly she felt about the bad situation. Only when she told them she planned to leave did they realize the need to act in her behalf. But then she reconsidered, and she gave them time to move her into a new position with potential to advance where no woman had ever been. That made her a winner in the eyes of top management. "The way she managed a nonsupportive boss distinguished her. It was a crisis time in her career—she was fed up and wanted out, but she stuck with us, absorbed the heat, continued to seek help. She showed sensitivity to the organization." She was seen as tough, loyal, willing to cope for the good of the company. "She sought advice, didn't combat the bad boss. It showed she trusted us, she was on the team."

How others saw this executive had as much to do with her success as did her own view of herself or even her documentable achievements. She created an image for herself—as a people-oriented manager and as a team player—that helped her get things done and be given new opportunities. She came to realize that friends in the right places and a certain amount of savvy were indispensable. Her difficult boss could have ended her career in the company. An important lesson for her was: "You need to know how to play the games. You must be political to get ahead. This is more important at higher levels than at lower ones."

Lesson 2: Take Control of Your Career

You can't always rely on the natural processes of the system. You can't rely on a mentor. No one is going to take care of you.

Your career is your responsibility—that's the rule that many executives, both women and men, use to guide their actions. Consciously and deliberately shaping your career is an important part of executive development for anyone, but it is more important for women because of the additional pressures on them. Women still encounter active resistance from colleagues and many family obligations that make career control more important—and more difficult.

Men are expected to have a career, but many women have had to realize sometime during their life that they would *like* a career, or that it was even a possibility.

I never thought of myself as a career person. I was dating a guy, and I didn't want to get promoted before he did. I told my boss, "Please don't promote me yet." My career didn't matter to me then, yet I worked terrifically hard. I succeeded in spite of myself!

The men and women in our studies realized in their thirties that they needed to take control of their careers; the realization, for both groups, occurred when they were being blocked or set back in their jobs. The men reacted when they were passed over for a promotion or when they discovered that they had been trapped in a dead-end job. They often took aggressive action that won them the result they wanted:

In research and development, I was amazed when I wasn't hired for a supervisory position. I quit the company and reapplied. You have to take some risks. I got to choose my job with the company [a supervisor in engineering]. Now I'm division president.

I thought I was passed over for a job during the reorganization, so I threatened to quit and began looking for a job. I was given a great job in Europe. . . . I was in my element. I was later brought back as vice president.

The executive women also experienced similar situations, but their wider array of career problems fueled their need to take their career by the scruff of the neck and drag it forward. Women's career problems included not only being passed over or left on the shelf, but also being banned from certain jobs, not receiving equal pay for equal work, and myriad other factors that they saw as overt discrimination and had to handle by themselves. The appropriate tactics weren't obvious; corporate norms might allow fast-track men to fight and fume to move their career along, but corporate expectations of women, as noted earlier in this chapter, were more confining. All of the 76 female executives had been in situations where they felt people were uncomfortable with them because they are women. Many felt they would be in higher positions if they were men. One executive said, "I suppose there were other promotions I was not considered for because I seemed a greater risk. The head of my division now is not real comfortable with me, probably because I'm female, and he doesn't know what to do with me." However, 29 (38.2 percent) mentioned that they faced and often fought distinct acts of discrimination, such as denial of pay, hiring or promotion, educational opportunities, or challenging assignments.

Some women put everything on the line and confronted management. One woman in her early thirties chose to have a showdown when she detected sex discrimination:

I was killing myself in that job—working very hard, doing work for the field guys and sitting on eight task forces. I was sitting in my boss's office, making $32,000 a year, when his boss blows into the office and says, "I've looked at that stuff on that young man, and $29,000 [as a starting salary] is OK." I was to train that young man. I wore the linoleum off the kitchen floor that weekend, and then I called my boss and said, "We have a problem. I want an 8:00 A.M.

appointment." On Monday morning, I had to threaten suit. I said that by the standards of any reasonable outside observer, this would be unacceptable. I hated to do that.

She finally obtained her salary increase six months later, but she had confronted her boss only after considerable thought. Others in similar situations who realized they had to exert more control over their career elected to make their contributions and their goals known in a less combative way.

As we noted earlier, managing people and getting the right kind of job are two crucial accomplishments that women must tackle if they want to move up in the corporation. Yet these two opportunities are more difficult to find if you're a woman. Women have to wait longer for a position with supervisory responsibilities. Twenty-nine was the median age at which our executive women got their first management job, whereas it was less than twenty-five for men. "A management job came to me much later than for my male peers," said one executive who, except for a short time supervising one employee, started her management career at age thirty-three with sixty subordinates. Four women became vice president at the same time they became manager.

Women often faced opposition when they tried to escape the velvet ghetto of staff jobs and move into the line-operating positions, the high-visibility, high-credibility jobs where they would have responsibility for profit and loss. Some executives had to go to great lengths to make the switch:

After the merger, the middle layer of management was superfluous. It became evident that we'd have to change jobs or lose them. One option I had was to go into the human resource department. I would have become the only woman at that level in the combined organization. But I was tired of personnel work.

Others didn't know what to do with me. The option I said I wanted was a two-step backward move into a line job. I never thought I'd run into redlining, but here it was: line management was off-limits to me. *I was so frustrated I cried in front of the head of all the company's operating groups.*

Although frustrated enough to cry—an act that might have damaged her image—this executive didn't give up. She cleverly figured out how to get a shot at the job she wanted, talking the fellow who had that job into going to a prestigious executive program and convincing senior managers to let her take his place.

Other executives dug their heels in and took the heat when they were offered a staff job instead of what they really wanted:

I had to battle to get a line job and establish my credibility. When I was ready to leave personnel, corporate set me up for staff interviews. I'd been in staff jobs for six years, and I knew (and my husband kept telling me) that I needed a line job. I ended up turning down a staff promotion. Everyone stopped talking to me. They thought I'd take the job. They had already hired my replacement! I went two and a half months without knowing what I'd be doing. Everyone was suspicious. I had to convince the head of the line department to take me. Then I faced open insubordination from a man who thought he'd been the best choice for the job. He challenged me openly, and I let it go on longer than I should (six months). This was terribly disruptive to everyone in the department. I already had to prove myself to everyone, and with this on top of it, it was very tough.

Getting into the business mainstream was a key career move for the female executives, perhaps much more important than the increase in salary. It's not surprising that, like the men, some women took an extremely aggressive stand in getting what they wanted:

After starting in market research, I decided that I wanted to be "where the action was," in account management. I have a good head and I'm good with people, so I didn't see any reason why I couldn't do it. I asked a friend, "How do you get into account management?" I was told to go to the personnel department and tell them I wanted to be an account manager. I saw the personnel guy, but he didn't take me seriously. I was sitting in a chair with my legs crossed, while he stood there and looked me up and down and then said, condescendingly, "What makes you think you can be an account manager?" I looked him straight in the eye and said, "Because I don't think with my legs." The guy turned red and was taken aback. He decided I was worth giving a shot. I was successful and later became vice president.

Being so aggressive, however, is obviously not always the best way to approach a career roadblock. Some executives got onto the fast track by massaging the system rather than clubbing it. One woman went for that all-important management experience when she changed her career in her midthirties, but her strategy called for hard work and patience along with some chutzpah:

I'd come to the corporation wanting to get into supervision. I gave myself five years. After four years, I got discouraged—it looked like it wouldn't happen. So I told myself, "I've got nothing to lose," and I got aggressive. When I didn't get invited to meetings, I went anyway. I didn't let myself get interrupted. I was promoted, but I still wasn't a supervisor. But then a committee was formed, and my peers chose me to chair it. From that position, I was able to put together some programs, plus I was doing well professionally (a patent). When a management position came open, I got it.

Executives have successfully used a variety of techniques to take command of their career. Some changed companies or industries, and some even changed their specialty in order to increase their chances of doing what they wanted to do. Some pushed their way up . . . and some pulled themselves *down* the ladder for a better shot at the top, or because of family commitments. Within all these different approaches to career management are a few guidelines that should help women succeed:

1. *Go for the "right" jobs as early as possible.* Certain line jobs and management experience are valuable commodities, and the road to the top usually requires them. These jobs differ from company to company, and finding out which jobs are important takes a great deal of observation and help from others. Once they are targeted, you must plan a strategy for getting the job that will be successful in your particular company.

2. *Control your career the best way you know how.* No single approach is the best, and nothing you do will always work. Expect setbacks, and choose the tools that feel right at the time. Your own needs, your knowledge of the company, and your judgment of the probability of success are all at the root of taking control.

Certainly there are some things everyone can do to make themselves more promotable, such as gaining new skills, training someone to be ready to replace you, and leveraging job interviews to learn about other parts of the business and to let people see your marketability. But preparing for career opportunities is only part of the story. Many executives must go after specific positions with urgency and precision, and that is where the greater risk lies. The maxim is often true: no guts, no glory.

3. *Ask for what you want.* As one executive advised:

Ask questions about opportunities and advancement. If you make people a little nervous, that's good—they'll move you more quickly. . . . Don't wait for a white knight to come charging along and notice you.

Because of stereotypes, senior management may assume that women don't want or cannot handle key jobs. Without information to contradict those assumptions, development and progress can come to a screeching halt. Myriad assumptions that "men don't have to deal with" can interfere with just getting the current job done, which affects career potential, as one executive discovered:

There was a task force put together that I heard about just by accident. I was the logical person to run it, so I didn't understand why I hadn't been told about it. I went to tell them I wanted to be part of it. . . . It required extensive traveling, and because I was married, they assumed I wouldn't be willing to be away from home (or my husband wouldn't let me). I told them that was between my husband and me and, in the future, not to try to make those decisions for me.

4. *Avoid derailment traps.* There are trade-offs in every executive's career. Sometimes fighting for your due is essential to get ahead, as many of these stories illustrate. At the same time, it is wise not to lose sight of the fact that your superiors have a vested interest in your movement. Fighting too much or over the wrong things could get you labeled as one who wants too much, a deadly flaw according to savvy insiders.

Using the resources available to control your career makes good sense, but that senior executives manage their resources—including your career—the way they see fit is also true:

You don't always get to take a job you like. Sometimes you take a job where senior management feels you can apply skills and move up.

Coming up with a blend of techniques to manage their career is what allowed some executives to keep their upward momentum. One woman was asked by her boss, his boss, and the CEO to take a new job, but she turned them down because she liked her present job and wasn't sure she liked the man who would be her new boss. The CEO asked her to reconsider, and she again turned it down. The CEO came to her a *third* time to ask her to take the job. To quell her fears, he guaranteed that she could return to her business unit anytime within two years if she decided it wasn't working out.

Some people may think this woman was crazy to reject the CEO's offer twice, but her experience with executives in previous jobs, whom she described as manipulative and sexist, probably made her doubt the wisdom of accepting advice. (She had felt forced to quit her job with two companies previously.) However, she recognized the importance of cooperating with the CEO:

In corporations, you have to do what they "ask" or they'll let you vegetate. I'd always managed my own career—even if I didn't always do a good job. All of a sudden, I was letting someone else decide what was best for me. It was a real leap of faith.

As we suggested earlier, faith may be what senior executives are looking for in a team player, instead of someone always looking out for herself. Clearly, neither path alone is likely to lead to success for anyone. The blend includes individual career cultivation along with a healthy dose of what is tolerated in a given corporate culture.

Lesson 3: Build Confidence

"She's comfortable with success—she doesn't need to prove herself every day." Confidence is an important characteristic in an executive. People expect to see confidence in top executives— they notice it, and they look for it. When savvy insiders described successful women and men, confidence and self-esteem arose often. Part of the "impressive image" cited for successful executives was the appearance of confidence. It seems that executives are impressive and, to some extent, easy to be with at least partly because others see them as having confidence in themselves.

Self-confidence is an enabling characteristic, a means to an end for many executives. It allows them to charge ahead, to risk, to take on the unfamiliar, and so on. True self-confidence may be a key to one's willingness to listen to feedback, to admit mistakes, and to accept fallibility along with one's strengths. Self-confidence is particularly important for women aspiring to executive heights, because image seems to play a bigger role in how women are evaluated and women must counter the popular view that they are not as confident as men and not as willing to take risks.

Some people have argued that direct experience, or success itself, is the most powerful source of confidence. It works like this: A manager succeeds at something and, as a result, becomes more confident and willing to take risks. The manager then takes on something that is more difficult and, with confidence, again succeeds. Success breeds confidence and risk taking, which, in turn, breed more success.

Of the key experiences that male executives described as building their confidence, nearly half were challenging assignments and promotions that increased the scope of their job. Since some types of assignments are off-limits to women or come later, women may need to be more creative or dramatic to earn confidence-increasing opportunities. Just as women need to take control of their careers to move ahead, they also have to actively seek out the experiences that will build their confidence.

The women executives in our study built their confidence in several ways:

1. *They took on a risky new job and performed well in it.* A big increase in management responsibilities was tied most frequently to increased confidence for women, although successful career change—an even more dramatic professional leap—was a close second. Perhaps women need to break out of their field more often than men to find the kind of challenge they need to feel good about their achievements.

One executive took on an operations department that was in chaos—her first management job, with six employees. The problems she faced included negative attitudes, low morale, overlapping responsibilities among workers, and unfinished work. Her boss told her to "fix it." It seemed overwhelming, at first, but she did it. And her confidence grew because she had evidence of her abilities. She was fortunate to get the chance to succeed in such an obvious way, more fortunate than many women. Only 3 other women of our 76 reported ever having dealt with a "fix-it" situation. Since 13 of the 79 executives in the men's study reported at least one "fix-it," it appears that this type of assignment is off-limits to many women. This disparity was also found for other types of challenging assignments, such as starting something from scratch or overseas travel.

Such assignments may become more available to female managers as they continue the corporate climb. The women in our study were younger on average than the men in the previous study, and some assignments seemed to be given to men fairly late in their careers, so it may simply be a matter of time. On the other hand, there is some evidence that women aren't offered the same opportunities as men no matter what age they are.

2. *They had helpful bosses who encouraged risk taking.* The chance to go it alone, sometimes with advice and direction from an encouraging boss, helped these executives develop. "He forced me to do things I wouldn't have done on my own" is how one executive described the effect of such a boss. Another executive described her boss in a similar way:

His management style changed me. He is so busy . . . his [other] responsibilities take 80 percent of his time, so [the department] is left in our hands, with all the good and the bad that comes. There is responsibility and work load far beyond an equivalent position. There is no time to hesitate, or to worry—you just do it. That has changed dramatically my approach, my level of self-confidence, and the number of things I've accomplished. I charge ahead. I was project-oriented, passive, hesitant, and cautious. I probably didn't have the self-

confidence to pick up the ball and run with it. I discovered all sorts of things I could do out of necessity, as I wouldn't have with anyone else. You can do almost anything you have to do.

One executive's helpful boss gave her behind-the-scenes coaching and then sent her out to do a job with the clear expectation that she could pull it off:

My boss told me, "Listen. The vice chairman doesn't know what he's doing. You're going to have to make the decision. Just go in there and state the facts, and then don't pause—*go right ahead and make a recommendation." I did that, and it worked.*

Other executives mentioned that a boss offering them a challenging job or project had signaled to them that their skills were highly regarded and they were expected to succeed. One executive on a track in the finance area was caught by surprise at age forty when her boss asked her during an annual performance review if she wanted a certain job reporting directly to the president, a job that was reserved for high-potential managers. "I'd never thought of myself as high-potential before. It made me look at everything differently, knowing I was able to progress that high." The encouragement that some women received from people they trusted and respected clearly affected how they saw themselves. The faith of others led them to have faith in themselves, and to take risks that they otherwise would have declined.

3. *They were exposed to a broad range of managers and found that they often compared favorably.* Through observing and getting to know others, the executives discovered to their great delight that they had some of the same characteristics as those they admired. They also learned that their skills, knowledge, or values sometimes exceeded those of others who were equally as successful as, or more successful than, they. If others with those limits can make it, they reasoned that they could progress toward the top as well.

Moving into a corporate staff position is one way to get a quick education in what executives are like. Both women and men who did this soon saw that those they had idolized from afar may have had some real strengths, but they were also just people like themselves. This was often their first exposure to senior executives, and some were surprised by how well they stacked up against their heroes. They felt better about their management capability and their abilities in general as a result:

As I moved higher in the company and became more involved in highly visible projects, I began to attend policy-making meetings with the senior VPs and the chairman. We often are involved with troublesome issues, but I soon saw that the group generally makes good decisions. I've gained a great deal of confidence by seeing that I can hold my own in their decision-making processes.

Taking courses is another way to meet other executives and see what they're really like. This was a primary source of self-confidence lessons for the men in our previous study. Not as many women described seminars or education programs as key events for themselves, but nearly half of those who did said their confidence increased as a result:

When I was about thirty-three, I spent several days at a management style course for executives. I had a liberal arts background and no management training. I was the only woman there, with fifty-year-old CEOs and tough engineers who'd never worked with a woman executive. During the course, we were constantly tested and videotaped. Several of the solutions I led my team toward were far better than anyone else's, and I learned I was probably the most innovative of the bunch. When one of the engineers cried, I realized I was as tough as or tougher than some of the men.

Another woman who participated in a similar program came to appreciate her weaknesses as well as her strengths, and her confidence changed the way she dealt with people:

Before I got my MBA, I thought I could do anything. But once at Harvard, I saw people who were functionally excellent at what they do. I saw people with incredible financial skills. From this experience, I realized that I am suited only for certain things. My interpersonal skills are my strength, and I wouldn't trade that for anything. I became more comfortable with myself—with my own unique blend of strengths and weaknesses—and I am more patient with my staff now. I realize people can't be good at everything.

4. *They became successful at outside activities.* Executives who wore out or became fed up with their job sometimes turned to community work, hobbies, physical fitness, or family relationships to reassure them that they are competent and likable people who are contributing to the betterment of humanity. Especially when women felt stagnant—coping with a stale job, for example, or being stuck with a boss who didn't challenge them—they relied on outside activities to boost their self-image. One executive mentioned that the writing and lecturing she did outside of her job was rewarding to her and "helps if things aren't going well at work." Another executive said she went and looked for another job offer, just to be sure of her marketability. Others found the leeway to experiment in community activities, which brought the satisfaction they were looking for:

I had been in my job so long, it had become easy. It was time-consuming, but I could do it with my eyes closed. I felt I needed to channel my energy, so I got involved in community work—chairing a women's career-planning organization. At work, the only acceptable management style has been a formal, discipline-oriented one. But I found, in the community group, a low-risk environment for trying out a coaching style of management. I eventually had the strength of will to use my new style back at work and, despite conflict with my boss's style, I was able to establish a new climate. I learned I could experiment outside the company and then use that to create an environment which is positive. I could do it!

The insight and reinforcement many of the executive women received from other people and organizations were substitutes for certain clear-cut success experiences that were not available to them on the job. Substitutes aren't adequate in themselves, we believe—women also have to experience career success to be truly confident in themselves.

Many aspects of effective executive behavior hinge on self-confidence. The cocky manner and arrogance that savvy insiders condemned in executives who derailed existed because they had too little self-confidence, *not* because they had too much. Ability to envision oneself as a senior executive is the key to getting there. With the vision *and* some traditional skill-building and other preparation, the goal is even more attainable. Self-confidence can help foster both. The executive whose boss asked her if she wanted that job reporting to the president gained confidence and took action once she realized how high she could go:

It gave me a different perspective. As I dealt with senior management, I put myself in their shoes and asked myself, "How would I handle this problem?" I became more political. I built a network with a give-and-take approach. My boss also told me, "Keep a list of good people in your drawer at all times." It's critical to a manager to have a strong staff. I began thinking that I should invest in the future.

She did that ten years before she talked to us. By the time we met her, she had worked her way up to become a senior vice president in charge of six hundred people.

Lessons for Success II
It's Not Enough to Work Smart

CHAPTER 5

The executive women in our study learned that working hard wasn't enough. They learned that they would have to steer their career purposefully in a positive direction to break the glass ceiling in their corporation. Their hard work had to be channeled, and they had to be smart about how they worked. But there was more: No matter how smart they were about their jobs and their business, they had to put themselves into a larger context. They could never be so smart that they wouldn't need other people. And knowing the rules didn't make unnecessary setting their own rules and, at times, challenging the system they had taken great pains to understand.

Finally, these executives learned (and are still learning) that the most important choices they make have nothing to do with intelligence or finding the correct solution. The biggest choices are the personal ones about how they want to lead their lives and how they define success. As women in nontraditional roles in a still-traditional society, they are forced to make choices that exclude some of their needs and wants, and they must live with what they choose.

Lesson 4: Rely on Others

One executive said that she'd had three mentors for whom she had worked. One was her boss early in her career:

He protected me and supported me. When he was sick for a couple of months, he gave me as much of his responsibility as [his peers] would allow.

Another boss she described was "a consummate politician who never did or said anything off-the-cuff." He was available to coach and advise:

He's a terrific manager. He used a lot of positive reinforcement. He was always very approachable. When I had to come to him for something I needed help with, he never made me feel embarrassed.

Her present boss was the third mentor, from whom she learned by watching his management style:

He has an emotional style—very friendly, catches people up with his enthusiasm. . . . He can bring people to consensus, but he's also very controlling. My style is much more task-oriented . . . I always want to do the right thing, and I always want my subordinates to be right, too. I'm still trying to reach a balance on the best way to handle it when they're not. My boss can yell and pound his fist on the table, because he has an emotional style. I can't yell—it wouldn't be accepted. I don't want to be a bitch, but I don't want to be a cream puff, either.

This boss is not only a role model for her, but also a sponsor:

Aside from getting me this job, if there's bad news, he elects to deliver it himself, and if it's good news, he makes sure I get credit.

To be successful, executives must rely on many other people. They need others' help to get the job done and to receive recognition for it, to obtain good assignments, to learn how the system works, to gain acceptance, and to cope with the pressures on them. Because different people are able and willing to provide only certain kinds of assistance (and perhaps only for a limited period of time), a number of executives recommended strongly that women develop a broad network of supporters rather than rely on any one person. This network can move executives along, but it also provides the all-important feedback on performance and on how an executive is perceived by others in the company.

As we have seen, savvy insiders believe that help from above is crucial to an executive. Higher-level managers, even up to the chairman, are sources of various kinds of help for executives. Seventeen of the 76 executives said they'd had a mentor, and another 16 said they'd had a sponsor or advocate. Although a few executives we interviewed reported that they received an array of benefits from a single person, most executives came to rely on several individuals or groups, each for a different sort of help. That is, a boss may have shared technical knowledge, while another senior executive recommended her for promotion. Some executives were helped simply by watching someone at work:

A key experience for me was observing the division president while I worked for him. He was brilliant; he would cut through the bureaucratic junk and confront people. He was a master psychologist, and he knew the business. By watching him, I learned to involve everyone in a problem-solving process, to confront, to listen, and to make sure there always are winners on all sides.

Management of subordinates is an often-mentioned factor in success and derailment because an executive must rely on them to get the job done. One of the most important realizations in an executive's career is that her or his main responsibility is to enable others to do the job. This typically is realized shortly after moving into one's first management position or a job that is significantly bigger than the preceding ones:

I moved from supervising [a technical] organization (where I had gotten the job because of professional competence) to general research manager. I had to leave being a professional expert because the people who worked for me were more technically competent than I was. I became more of a manager rather than a technician. Goal-setting and building a team became important. My job changed from getting individual recognition for my technical competence to getting other people to do their work.

Learning *how* to manage people was reported more often by executives, both female and male, than any other type of lesson. It's hard, it's complicated, and it's crucial. Learning to manage people usually means managing subordinates, but getting others to cooperate was also important, according to our executives. As the jobs got larger, their reliance on other people grew. Savvy insiders weren't the only ones to recognize the importance of working with others as a factor in success.

Some people we talked to about our research said they believe that women find it harder than men to let others do their jobs, to take a "hands-off" approach to managing. However, making that switch from a do-it-all-myself technical role to delegating work was a challenge that executive men confronted as well. Women generally do have more staff jobs that require carrying out technical work, and women are thought of as being "detail-oriented," but neither of these factors seems to have a strong effect on management style. All executives must learn that managing is not so much doing it yourself as letting, encouraging, and helping others do the job.

Most executives we interviewed realized quickly that their subordinates could make or break their own career, and also that their authority over their subordinates was full of holes. They could hire and fire people, but what happened in between was related less to formal authority than to their ability to understand and influence their people. This point hit home with some women when they got a subordinate who was incompetent or hostile, sometimes apparently only because they were women. The damage such a subordinate can do to productivity and morale pushed some to act and to change the way they managed:

A man who reported to me was incredibly duplicitous. He would attribute bad motives to me so that the people who worked for him would be too scared to come to me to complain about him. *He was an out-and-out liar. He would play mind games on me, telling me that people were whispering behind my back. Finally, things got so bad that several people who did report to him came to me. I realized then that we were all being manipulated, and I got rid of him.*

Female executives need to acquire support outside as well as inside the company. Sometimes a sanity check is necessary— to get reassurance of one's skills and worth when life at the office becomes discouraging. Support from family and friends can help relieve the stress and strain that executives face day after day.

Managing others' perceptions of them, since stereotypes and expectations abound, is critical for women. They must also get straight performance feedback—to learn what they are good at, along with what to improve and how. Women seem to be at a disadvantage in both regards. Constructive feedback is a rare commodity for anyone in a corporation, but generally the women we interviewed believe they receive even less than men.

Without feedback, corrections can't be made and problems on the job can escalate until they are beyond repair. One executive worked for a while for a "two-faced, rotten manager" who kept refusing to give her any negative feedback. He told her she was doing a great job, but she heard differently through the grapevine. He waited until her annual performance review to hammer her with criticism, and then she quit. If she had it to do over, she would have given herself a better chance:

I can't change his personality, so I should have figured out a way to get feedback from him. The fact was, we had a serious disagreement about how [the project] should be channeled, and neither one of us was willing to confront it."

A number of the 76 executives weren't willing to accept a lack of feedback; they took the initiative:

I think people are reluctant to give me—or any woman—negative feedback. They'll take a more indirect approach, as if they're not sure I can take it. But I always insist on it. If a person won't volunteer criticism, I ask what they didn't like about the job I did.

When their boss wasn't a good source of feedback, they took advantage of the feedback they received from others in their network:

One day, I had lunch with a male peer. He said, "No one likes working with you. No one wants to work on your projects. I'm telling you this as a friend." That wiped me out. I went to the john and got hysterical for a half hour. Then I talked to my supervisor. She gave me support, but the wrong kind—she denied the information, telling me, "They're wrong, you're right."

A couple of days later, I started to cry while getting dressed—I didn't want to go to work. My husband asked me what was wrong, and I began to realize what was happening. There was strain at home because my job had turned into a career, and I was earning more than my husband, and we weren't talking much. I felt totally responsible for the kids, and he was working late a lot.

At work, I was really managing the department, but my boss didn't tell anyone I was in charge. I had the responsibility but not the authority, so I was seen as too domineering. I wasn't letting people make mistakes; I was intervening too soon. Because of the strain at work and at home, I was too controlling. You have to let people do for themselves, then help them figure out the mistakes when they ask. That's one of the toughest transitions to make.

Another executive sought feedback from a different group when she felt stymied:

My new boss and I have very different styles, and that caused me to question my own style. I had lunch with my former subordinates. They reinforced me—they had strong feelings about the effectiveness of my management style. It was a boost of confidence for me. I decided to go back to my natural style—it works best for me and is effective. My subordinates helped me get back on the track, and I learned it's all right for me to be who I am.

Feedback is valuable information for anyone trying to learn and grow in a profession. Soliciting and acting on feedback is also a good strategy for defusing opposition from colleagues while getting the benefit of their wisdom. If male executives find it easier to accept into their ranks women who ask for their guidance, then that interaction is even more valuable for the bridge it creates between up-and-coming women and top management.

Women must prove their own abilities in corporations, of course, but the need for a strong support system as well is undeniable. Successful executives have made tough choices about how much assistance to accept and from whom. These are difficult judgment calls because, on one hand, senior executives expect you to trust them, and on the other hand, entrusting your career to someone else can be dangerous. The women we interviewed did not always make the right choice, but they learned from their experiences and sharpened their sense of who will help them and who will hurt them.

Lesson 5: Go for "the Bottom Line"

I was the first woman union superintendent for my company. I worked on the shop floor. The typical person in this job was a man who had risen through the ranks and was a former union member. I was young, had an MBA, and was a woman. So any proposals I made were unacceptable to the union—partly because of me. Over time, I came to recognize the other side of the issues and began to negotiate in ways that neither the union nor I had done before. I learned to be tougher, and we gained concessions on the union's power. But I also learned what and when to compromise (or give up) when things being sought were unreasonable. Negotiation is hard work, and I often wondered why I got myself into the job. There was physical danger—people had knives and flourished them as I walked through. And I was working for a nincompoop and had problems at home, too.

Toughness is necessary for anyone to handle the pace and complexity of management positions. Women may have to go farther than men to demonstrate a hard-nosed approach to business and a thick skin in order to be considered a serious executive contender—the men in charge may have preconceived notions that women are not tough enough. The ability to take charge and do what is best for business had to be learned by the executive women and adequately demonstrated in a variety of ways.

1. Getting Results

As a product manager, I was given a very large business to run—a business that was under competitive attack. Someone else had introduced a product, and we'd been sleepy. We could catch up or lose out within one or two seasons. I realized that if I tried to work within *the bureaucracy, we were doomed to failure. I got agreement (from top management) on broad strategy, then I went ahead. When I took over the business, sales were in the $90–$100 million range. Today, sales are $400 million. I've learned I must figure out what needs to be done and do it, even getting approval later, if necessary. It's important to stand up to management and tell them what is right, instead of what they want to hear.*

Accountability is a concept that came alive for many executive women when they took on a job with new responsibilities. They learned quickly that making the bottom line is a prerequisite for any successful business career.

One thirty-nine-year-old executive, who had been a manager for thirteen years and had managed as many as 350 people, was dealt a significant blow because she let her attention wander from the bottom line:

Last year I didn't get a merit bonus for the first time. I was devastated. My efforts were great, but the results could have been better. . . . I learned that working hard doesn't always bring rewards. The results have to be there, too.

Executives are accountable for what they *can* do, but they are also responsible for knowing what they *cannot* do. This may be particularly difficult for women, because they are under enormous pressure to do outstanding things all the time:

I got a promotion that made me responsible for selling work to people within the company. My boss told me about a part of the company that wanted a sales measurement/forecasting system. We could hire a summer computer student who could put together the program, and all I had to do was sell it. Well, I sold it (that was my job), and then we found we couldn't do it. They actually wanted a simple answer to a complex problem. It was awful. We should have stopped the project after a month when we realized we were in over our heads. We didn't ask for help and we should have. We all suffered.

Discovering what the bottom line is, as important as it is, may be the easy part. Often, what executives have to do to get results is scary and unpleasant, particularly when it comes to confronting subordinates. Our studies of both male and female executives revealed that executives dreaded a situation in which one or more of their people had to be let go to improve the bottom line. Of all the tough demands on them, executives tended to procrastinate on this kind of responsibility more than on any other. It is the "dirty work" of management that can't be delegated. The manager must weigh the welfare of the employees against the benefit to the business, and the solution isn't always evident, since a manager has obligations to all parties. Learning how to juggle those obligations makes some managers stand out:

I was twenty-nine when the company I was working for was close to going out of business. It was clear to me that my actions would keep the company going. There was one bad piece of news after another. I had to be optimistic for my crew, working all those hours all the time. I confided in people outside the firm, asked for their opinions. My husband was helpful, he listened patiently. I didn't fear for my career but for others and the company. I knew they were depending on me, and that helped. I prided myself on being forthright with people, and I couldn't always be that way in this situation. It made me suffer that my own integrity was at risk.

In the end, I laid off two hundred people. It was an orderly retrenchment; I was proud of it. It was like war—people were loyal to me when they had no reason to be—I had to lay them off. I had to lay off a man in his fifties with three or four kids; I was almost in tears. He said, "I'll be fine, don't worry"—he actually laid himself off.

As we noted earlier, one of the most difficult situations faced by executive women is dealing with a problem employee who is also a minority. This is a potential minefield that tears at conflicting loyalties. In such situations, women are watched carefully by other executives, since resolution of the problem seems to be an important rite of passage.

Most of our executives ultimately let the minority employee go, but they seemed to handle the problem with sensitivity and located an alternate job for the employee whenever possible:

My company has an aggressive EEO policy, and I have a commitment to it. But we have a very small minority population, so we work hard to attract good minority candidates. There was some corporate pressure to hire a minority for an opening. He interviewed well; in fact, he was impressive. His personality and fit with the group met my expectations.

He couldn't do the work. After six months' probation, I went to management and told them I'd hired an unqualified person with unique interpersonal skills. I worked with management for months to identify another position that would be more appropriate, but I couldn't find him another job. We had priced him out of less skilled jobs, so I finally told him that he'd have to leave. I let him keep an office here until he could find a new job. . . . I found out that I was a gut-level manager—I focused on and reacted to him as a person at the expense of not putting him in the appropriate job. I felt personal responsibility for that year of his life. I finally realized that I can never do away with my gut, but my hiring decisions since then have been more cautious—I've learned to sort out my vested interests from what will serve the organization best. . . . I was honest with him about his performance, I got support from senior management, and I put in more time and stayed closer to the issue than someone else would have.

Women must be tough—at least as tough as their male colleagues—to get bottom-line results for the business. But making tough business decisions is not enough—they also must be willing to live with the consequences of their actions. Both women and men in our two studies learned that they had limits on what they were willing to do and on what they would tolerate.

2. Doing the Right Thing

To be successful, executives must ascertain what is necessary to ensure that they can do their job well and achieve the business objectives expected of them. They gauge themselves by the bottom line in their business unit or function. They go beyond that, however, to the underlying values of what good business practices are and how people should treat one another. The executives in our study took a stand not only so that they could do a better job, but also when they found what others were doing so offensive that they could no longer ignore it:

I worked for a woman who was planning to do a presentation but couldn't do it because of a religious holiday. She said she would put it together if I would do the presentation. I offered to come in over the weekend (the presentation was on the following Monday), but she said she had it under control. I decided to come in Sunday afternoon anyway, and nothing *was done. I worked all afternoon and evening—my husband even came in to make graphs for me—slapping something together. It was adequate but not good.*

I was furious *with her. I told her boss that I wouldn't work with her anymore. Shortly after this, I was promoted and transferred, so it didn't hurt me to refuse to work with her. I would* never *do that to someone. You're responsible for your work, and that's that.*

Taking action and charging ahead are important, but doing the *right* thing is equally important. Our executives sometimes had to take a stand for moral reasons, even if it meant jeopardizing their career:

There was a very intense political war between our group, which was given a challenging project to manage, and another group, left with only system maintenance to work on. The man I worked for, one of the most intelligent men I've ever known, felt we could solve the conflict. But just after we installed a state-of-the-art system, the other group tried to sabotage it. Their manager lied, cheated, and misrepresented our work, until my manager was forced to resign.

110

Another fellow and I decided not to let this happen. I made an appointment with the president and chairman of the board to tell my side of the story. I told him, "If this company is willing to let this happen, I won't work here anymore—I'll go wash dishes in a restaurant!" He said he believed me, but the decision had been announced and he couldn't change that. He also said he'd investigate my story. After that, the manager of the other group was fired.

I felt I had done the right thing, but at great cost. The man who had fired my boss was vice chairman of the board—it took me six years to recover. Two years ago, someone finally told me I had done the right thing. I couldn't have ignored it, but I put my whole career on the line. You have to deal with politics but not prostitute yourself.

For women struggling to fit into the corporate culture, making an issue of others' behavior isn't a good way to be accepted, of course. Generally, executives suggest that being noncontroversial and nonthreatening gains others' acceptance and approval. But an individual has to be able to live with herself. Certainly, taking on the chairman should not be done lightly, but that course of action should not be ruled out for fear of reprisal.

3. The Personal Bottom Line

All people have a personal bottom line with regard to their priorities and ethics as well as their achievements, and it is the ultimate gauge of success. One executive did a superb job of fitting into her company—she had become a senior vice president by the time she was interviewed—but we have to wonder whether she lost track of her own bottom line in the pursuit of another:

When I interviewed with the company, I had had a very successful interview, but I lied my way through it. It worked, but I was pretending to be something I wasn't, and now I was stuck with the results. I was able to pull it off, but I don't know how much that says for the company. Corporate life is a game. Results don't always matter if you know how to play the game well enough.

Choosing where and how much to fit in is part of the challenge executives face. As one executive learned, sometimes it's best for you if you stop trying to fit in, but that doesn't mean you have to sacrifice everything:

When I moved into a new department, it was a matter of fitting in without hating myself. Those I would work with were a bunch of smug bastards. They didn't pay attention to how people felt. I learned that if you don't share some values, you're going to be miserable if you try to fit in. Fitting in is a poor goal. Getting people to trust you and cooperate with you is a good goal.

Clearly, there is danger in assuming that meeting tough business goals is the only requirement for success, just as there is danger in not concentrating enough on the results needed in the job. As in other phases of their careers, successful executive women need to find the right balance between being tough and being human:

I was seventeen years into it before I was appointed supervisor of nine men . . . I saw myself as warm and friendly, but when working with people who had been coworkers, it's more difficult to establish new roles. A consultant gave me the advice to be tough 5 percent of the time, and the other 95 percent will take care of itself. When you have to make a decision, face it, make it, and take action. This advice gave me the strength to be myself and not worry over every issue, just the important ones.

Lesson 6: Integrate Life and Work

One executive had been through a major financial crisis when she was out of work, unable to find a job. She was also forced to take a job she didn't want when a merger eliminated the job she had held and liked. But she said these challenges paled in comparison to one:

The overriding challenge for me was juggling parenting and my career over those years, trying to do well at both, trying to grow in a career without crippling the children. It was difficult to live with the guilt. It was difficult finding time and energy, putting one or the other off. As a single parent, I wanted a career, and I couldn't rationalize that it was to provide for the family.

A number of women commented that living a full life is more challenging and more difficult for female executives than it is for their male colleagues. When comparing themselves to men, many resent the trade-offs only they have to make. Some believe that they have to put more time and energy into their career than do men. Many women also find that they have major responsibility for the household, maintaining a relationship, and child-rearing:

Most men here are married. They seem to think food magically appears in a refrigerator. They can't comprehend chores.

I add up the amount of time I spend with the kids, and I compensate. My husband doesn't do this. He will be out of town all week and then play golf on Saturday.

The fact that so many in our group want marriage or children suggests that these executives are not iron-minded workaholics as some would have us believe. They do have needs beyond their work that they try, sometimes desperately, to meet.

The needs and motives of these executive women don't make them different from their male counterparts. But for the women, pursuing their personal goals may be a riskier proposition. They are scrutinized more closely than men, and they are judged on their personal life as well as on their job performance. If they indicate to more senior executives that their personal life is important, the suspicion that it will take precedence over their career grows. And on the basis of that suspicion, a woman's performance may be suspect or her advancement slowed.

Attempting to balance their lives by developing a personal relationship outside of work or starting a family, then, can jeopardize these executives' career. For this reason, some executives sacrifice the personal side, while others juggle and trade off between them as best they can. Some eventually conclude that the compromises they must make in balancing their lives are too crippling and, for lack of a suitable alternative, trade in their executive status for a better personal life.

With few exceptions, the 76 female executives we interviewed made the decision that a number of savvy insiders consider to be a milestone in their successful careers—the "priority decision" to put their career first and squeeze in whatever else in life they can around it.

Clearly, it is important for any executive to be seen as committed to the job and the company. For women, it is more important that they visibly limit their family life and personal relationships to convince others that they are committed. That point is particularly salient in the cases of two derailed women, described by savvy insiders, whose relationships were frowned upon—one asked not to be transferred (or promoted) because she was seeing a man, and one became engaged to a man employed by a supplier to the company. And when savvy insiders pinpointed critical turning points in the careers of women as a group, the decision to put their career first was the most frequently cited.

The obvious solution for women who want to demonstrate their commitment to the corporation and thereby earn a chance for advancement into the executive suite is to give up everything else, including a family. Few of our executives found that solution acceptable. Only 5 of the 76 had never been married; the vast majority had tried to combine a family with their career. These women didn't believe that they would have to sacrifice significant personal relationships. Yet all of the executives had the challenge of weighing and juggling their personal and professional pursuits. As women, many of them were under constant strain as they tried to switch from one role to another. They felt pressure to conform to one role or another, without the freedom to combine them.

When we asked male executives about the biggest challenge they ever faced, only three of the nearly one hundred challenges they described had to do with personal events such as marriage or family. The women, however, cited more personal experiences than the men—nearly 20 percent—because of the choices that were involved for them.

Deciding not to have children, for example, can be a major factor in the "priority decision." One executive didn't think she was unique or handicapped by this choice:

I chose to not be married, to have no children. I am not a victim. I don't regret anything in my life—my marriage, divorce, decisions I made. I believe I can have whatever I want. For men, it's hard to say if it's different. They feel their children are growing up without them. Some regret not having a good intellectual relationship with their wife. They have their own set of trade-offs. Men aren't all that happy.

About a dozen executives considered their deliberate decision not to have children a necessary sacrifice. Said one, age thirty-nine:

I gave up children. Two or three years ago, my husband had a vasectomy. I didn't want children. I'm going to be a career person. If I could do one more thing, I would have children, too. But I'm a career person.

Many more women are facing that choice now, in their thirties, well aware of the pros and cons but not eager to lock themselves in for the next thirty years:

I don't consider my divorce a "sacrifice," but I'm concerned about the children issue. I think this is the major difference between sacrifices made by men and women. There are two things I want to be able to look back and say I did—I want to have made a difference for women, and I want to have led a full life. I'm ambivalent right now. I want to concentrate on my career, but the biological clock is starting to tick down. I'm not sure I want children, but I don't want to regret not having them, when I'm sixty-five. I don't believe you can be a "superwoman." My friends who are combining a career and children don't seem to have any personal time, and I need personal time. They generally don't seem very happy. I don't mean that they regret having children, but that it's all just a little too much to handle. It would mean having to reprioritize my life, and I'm just not willing to do that right now.

There is no easy answer. The relief of having the children over with is often balanced by doubt or regret, yet the anxiety with which many women ponder the decision argues for post-poning the decision. The advice our executives gave included having a clear sense of your priorities so that you can get on with your life in whatever way you choose. But the choice about children is a formidable one, and some executives postpone it repeatedly until the choice is no longer theirs.

Those who did choose to have children sometimes planned the event(s) for a time when they felt they could slow down a bit in their career and devote themselves to pregnancy and child-rearing. But that strategy was also fraught with peril. One executive decided to get pregnant after a department head left, and her proposal to take over the department was refused for several months:

He told me he was hiring someone else—I'd have the same old boring job. If he'd said yes, I wouldn't have gotten pregnant. I would have been afraid it would cut into the new job. Part of why I got pregnant was that I was unhappy with my job.

After she had been pregnant for only a month, her staff grew from one to four, and the job grew considerably:

116

I had new, older, high-level people reporting to me for the first time. I had to run a whole department while I was throwing up. I had to train them—I knew I'd be gone for three months. I was so mellow, tired, sick, and happy about the baby that I didn't let my other instincts get in the way. I was supportive. My natural way is to be encouraging. I didn't have the energy to do anything else.

She did well at managing the department in the interim, and six months later she was promoted to head of the department. Her response?

I had always wanted it. But I didn't care now. I was focused on a child, family, being happy.

As was true for some other executives we talked to, her career had always come first, until she got the feeling that her advancement or career growth was blocked. Only then was she willing to turn to the personal arena for fulfillment. Once she had made the switch, her dream job followed. She couldn't refuse it, but she knew the demands on her to manage both at the same time would be extraordinarily tough.

A long-term marriage has eluded many of our female executives, in contrast to men. Nineteen percent were divorced or separated at the time of our interview, and another 11 percent had remarried. Not only are the time constraints of the executive job prohibitive, but the marital role requirements for women are seen very differently. It takes more to be a wife than to be a husband:

It's easier to be married to a wife than to a husband. Men don't get the same level of concern if they travel. There's more pressure on a woman's marriage. There are very few happily married women—on their first marriage—in executive positions.

Married executive women also have another problem that most other women do not have—their income is sometimes

more than their husband's, a factor that has damaged if not destroyed more than one marriage:

*There has been a real strain on our marriage which comes and goes. In
a previous job, my salary jumped much higher than my husband's.
Then he caught up. When I took my present job, the salary and
bonuses put me way above him again. He changed jobs in January
after four months of interviewing. He did this without telling me a
thing. My husband said one reason was that I did not think enough of
the people he had been associating with. I think the real reason is he
could become a partner one day and reach parity with me.*

Some executives have overcome these roadblocks by choosing the right partner, sometimes the second time around. But
they encounter problems, too. Finding time for the relationship
while being careful not to jeopardize one's business credibility
is difficult for women in particular:

*I'm single. It's very difficult to meet men who are not with the
company. I spend tremendous time at work, but work-related
relationships are off-bounds to me. I feel strongly about not doing
that. For men, it's easier to meet women. There's less of a taboo on
seeing women at work. There are more women junior to them in rank
or age.*

Those executive women who have managed to overcome
the problems associated with being married and raising children often find that having this "all" isn't enough. They miss
other aspects of life that often are available to their male
colleagues:

*I sacrificed time with friends, nurturing friendships. I lost that for so
many years. . . . Every minute, I was parenting when I wasn't
working. You can't work on friendships only every third year.*

Is it any wonder that some executives have stopped looking
toward the traditional, so-called "balanced" life as a model for

their own life? The view of career + marriage + children + some community voluntarism thrown in for good measure as the ultimate goal just doesn't add up the same way for many women. Often, when women put their career first, they prepare themselves to lose everything else. Some executives realized that they had to keep their personal life a secret, lest their colleagues jump to the conclusion that their priorities had changed.

Some deliberately try to convince their colleagues that their personal life is not important, or at least that it couldn't possibly interfere with their career. One executive pointed out that she doesn't talk about her kids at the office. Another executive kept news of her marital separation from everyone at work for months. She continued to wear her wedding ring and revealed no evidence that her personal life had changed so dramatically. Obviously, others must not have known enough about her personal life when she and her husband *were* living together to detect the difference. Like some others, she had protected her privacy and was able to disguise her personal life when necessary.

Sometimes it isn't possible to disguise personal events, and then the women we interviewed had to take their chances. Pregnancy is one of those undisguiseable situations. A few talked about how dreadful that is for executive women and how they endured the experience.

After years of trying to blend in and be as indistinguishable as possible from male managers to gain acceptance, women can find pregnancy a traumatic experience—one that makes a woman literally stand out. "It's the most female thing you can do," said one executive. The effect may have been especially shocking to women who didn't expect the treatment they received:

I'd like to write the executive's guide to having a baby. I have been stunned by paternalistic, well-meaning male executives. Their remarks made me really angry. I haven't been stereotyped in a long time! Their only experience with pregnant women is their wives. They asked me, "Why are you still here?" Of the top twenty-five executives, maybe only two of their wives have a serious career. I tried to see their concern instead of the prejudice. I wouldn't have believed this [before I got pregnant].

"It amazes me," one pregnant executive said. "At my level, people still ask me if I'm coming back to work." But it *is* difficult for some women on the fast track to come back after giving birth and act as if nothing has changed. Not everyone is like the executive who said she missed three weeks of work and was glad to be back: "I'm more at home at work. I'm not a good mom."

The difficulty of balancing the time demands and dealing with the stereotypic attitudes of colleagues causes some female executives to turn the other way—to their personal needs—for fulfillment. They look for give on the other end—they shed some work responsibilities, and career potential, when they sense that they cannot handle the additional demands of a baby:

It was a critical choice point—how to integrate a general management job with family life. I made a decision not to continue on a general management track and take a division with 2,500 people. Everyone tried to push me, but I said no. There are limits. . . .

Perhaps it is because some women have deserted the fast lane when confronted with such decisions that senior executives make the assumptions they do and expect the worst. There is, in fact, a level of risk to the corporation and to those who have made an investment in a high-potential female manager when she is confronted with the "priority decision." More than one woman in our group made a career shift to accommodate what they saw as the children's needs.

Each person sets her own standards and defines her own limits. And each chooses on that basis. The reason that most of our executives chose to go for both career and family (marriage and/or children) must revolve around their needs for personal gratification as well as career achievement.

The satisfaction of accomplishing the juggling act, or perhaps even just surviving from week to week, seems to hinge on understanding what is important to you:

You can't do it without some give-ups. You've got to make compromises along the way. You must have a sense of your priorities so you'll know where to make the compromises.

In fact, when a personal experience outside of work was cited as a key event by our executives—having children, a family change, or relocation—they often reported learning about their goals, what they really enjoy in life and in their work, and how to balance their needs. Their increased self-awareness also had a much more direct impact on their effectiveness as managers of time and of people:

Up until the birth of my first child three years ago, I'd always tried to keep my work and home life separate. For example, I would work late, but I wouldn't bring work home with me. But things would spill over anyway. After my child was born, I stopped putting up artificial boundaries. I admitted that everything had to fit into a twenty-four-hour day. That's all the time you've got. I brought work home with me, and I was more flexible about my hours. It gave me more time with my child, and I got more accomplished. Resentments I'd always felt in the past fell away. I managed better. My perspective on work had changed, and I could feel the difference.

I had to learn how to manage my housekeeper, because she had my son. I know I'm a good manager—if I weren't, I wouldn't be here—but at work, it's just me and my subordinates. In this case, my son was involved. If I made the housekeeper angry, she wouldn't confront me—she'd take it out on my son. It was a delicate balancing act to get her to do what I wanted her to do without making her resentful. I had to learn how to motivate her positively. The best way to do this is by getting the person to like what they're doing—to enjoy working. This is the clearest lesson about managing I've ever had. While I've learned from the men I've reported to, it was much more indirect.

Executives can and do learn valuable lessons from personal experiences, and that may be another reason that they try to squeeze so much into their lives. But they pay a steep price for trying to combine personal interests with their career, and many are well aware of that price. While men, in the advice they said they'd give younger managers, didn't often address how to handle personal aspects of life, the women covered it explicitly. Their advice was across the board—set priorities, balance, sacrifice, wait to have kids, and so on—reflecting their own individual needs and how they handled such situations in the past.

Choosing and juggling have been difficult for executive women. They have not come up with a solution suitable for female executives as a group, nor have some solved the problem for themselves. Balancing work and personal life is a problem that keeps arising for some, a problem they live with almost constantly. Eleven of our group said they want out of the corporate climb so they can meet their personal needs. Others aren't willing to go that far—at least not yet—but the options are tempting.

Breaking the Glass Ceiling
Making It to General Management

CHAPTER 6

She came to us from another company. She was recruited as the highest-level woman we had. Not long after we hired her, I had the opportunity to talk to her former boss at a cocktail party. "You knocked off a big one," he said. "She was one of the quickest studies I ever had—perceptive, bright, goal-oriented—and I hated to lose her!"

Soon after, we were in a policy meeting together. I heard her speak and watched her actions. She made an excellent first impression; she seemed to wear well. She was intelligent, bright. I had a very positive feeling toward her. I was really impressed with her ability to take a tough stand. Later, when her name was in for a higher-level slot, she won out easily over two men—she was balanced *all the way around.*

She makes her people important. She has a very open style and communicates clearly to subordinates. She's fair and therefore highly respected by people.

She has been able to work with lots of high-level people to get things done. The president is enamored of her and has given her lots of special attention. She has a great degree of elasticity, great cool under pressure. In fifty corporate settings, I've only seen her lose her cool two times—most would lose it one time out of five. She's very controlled. She would get as many strong votes [for higher executive positions] as anyone else.

Women in management have carried an enormous load. Many women have paid their dues, even a premium, for a chance at a top job, only to find a glass ceiling between them and their goal. The glass ceiling is not simply a barrier for an individual, based on the person's inability to handle a higher-level job; it applies to women as a group who are kept from advancing higher *because they are women.*

The glass ceiling may exist at a different level in different companies or industries, but just short of the general manager job often marks the glass ceiling for women in large companies. Even in the more progressive companies, it is rare to find women at the general management level.

The general management level also varies from company to company, but as a rule, it means taking responsibility for more than one type of business/function or more than one division's functions. Attaining this level represents a major transition in responsibility according to both the female and the male executives we interviewed, a transition so difficult that failure is a distinct possibility. Executives at the general management level may have an idea of what goes on in each area, but they are not expert in more than one or two, at most, of those areas. These positions are what some of our 76 executives called "real management" because accountability is broad and visible.

Women are often kept from general management. Perhaps this is because of the quantum leap in responsibility general management represents—many senior managers are unwilling to risk putting a woman where she might fail. They may doubt the ability of a woman to cope with such expansive or far-flung responsibilities, and they may fear the visibility a woman would have at such a level.

General management is also the point at which managers are admitted into the "club" at many companies, not unlike a community country club. Prospective members are reviewed carefully by a committee of current members and assessed on criteria that aren't always concrete, even though applicants must pay their dues. As in a country club, people lacking the proper background, image, sex, or whatever, can be blackballed.

Because of general attitudes toward women and the lack of familiarity many men have with executive women, the club is often closed to women. Despite the dues they have paid, women typically are not seen as appropriate members. They may be blackballed because the criteria go beyond professional abilities into the broader, but murky, area of compatibility. Men may not be comfortable around executive women. In her 1985 *Working Woman* article "The Breakthrough Generation: 73 Women Ready to Run Corporate America," Basia Hellwig reported that "studies have shown that top executives tend to promote people into leadership positions who are as much like them as possible," because "men are simply more comfortable with and seem to gravitate toward people like themselves. . . . Because of this, gender will be a barrier to women," according to 44 percent of the recruiters *Working Woman* interviewed.[1]

There are risk and discomfort associated with admitting women to the general management team. Another factor that may be involved in barring women from the club is the benefit package that often goes with the rank. Bonuses and special perks often accompany the general manager title and, to the extent that male executives may be reluctant to let women share in these symbolic rewards, they may foster even greater reluctance to bring women into the ranks. There are still some people who believe that women should be paid and otherwise rewarded less than men, which makes women a business bargain and, consequently, tolerable at least to a point.

Many talented female executives, then, are closed out before their time. The fact that *any* women make it into general management may be a minor miracle. Only a small number of women have broken the glass ceiling to enter general management. In our study of 76 executive women, we classified only 52 of them as general managers—the other 24 were one level below general manager. The most we interviewed from any one company was 7, and these are companies that may each have as many as three hundred or more general managers. There were some companies with more female general managers than we interviewed, but most of the companies in our study had only one or two women at that level.

The 52 general managers we interviewed had done what very few other women have been able to do—break through the glass ceiling. They were smart, worked hard, and achieved a great deal, but the same can be said of many other women who lose out on general management jobs even though they may be at least as motivated and capable. The women who entered general management seem to have some "extras" on their side that may have enabled them to break through.

From our research, we have identified three types of extras that the vast majority of general managers mentioned as they told us about their careers and their lives. These extras include credibility and presence, either outside the company or inside, often with a prestige connotation; the unusually strong advocacy of at least one influential person higher in the company; or pure luck that facilitated their career movement in some way. Fifty of the 52 general managers mentioned at least one of these extras, and 36 of the 52 mentioned having two or all three.

We know the savvy insiders believe that getting help from above can make the difference between success and derailment. Yet winning support and sponsorship from higher executives is terribly difficult because of the risks to executives if their female protégée bombs. Most executives want to get as close to a performance guarantee as possible before advocating a woman for general management. Credibility and prestige may be the extras that lead to other extras—getting active support from others or coming out ahead in a reorganization. The combination, then, of establishing credibility in special ways and having the support of influential people seems to give high-potential women enough ammunition to break through the ceiling. If that's not enough, the timing of opportunities may add the extra bit needed.

Extra 1: Credibility

Women in management still must prove their suitability for executive positions before they can be promoted into these jobs. Yet often the only acceptable evidence of suitability is to do the job successfully. This problem is a critical one for many women—a plight similar to that of the young graduate who cannot get job experience because all potential employers want someone with experience.

We have already noted that women need to be consistently outstanding to move ahead in their careers. The general managers in our group were able to build a case for their own competence so compelling that senior executives were convinced they would succeed. The risk to them as advocates of a woman was reduced to a tolerable level. These women built their case by demonstrating their professional abilities for the executives in person, or if they relied on the testimony of others, it was from other executives they respected.

Within the company, it was clear from the interviews, more than half of the general managers had worked directly with senior executives on a project or as an adviser on sensitive or confidential matters. Those who were in staff roles at the time advised top management on compensation practices, tax policy, speaking and public relations, and various other sticky issues. They were the experts from whom the executive committee sought counsel on everything from whom to hire or fire to what business to buy or sell.

The general managers had sometimes served on a task force that also involved senior executives as another way of having direct contact. These included women who were in line jobs at the time, as well as in staff jobs, since those in line jobs could be experts in such areas as cost-cutting or the ins and outs of a new region where they were in charge.

In both these types of roles that required expertise, the women executives acted as problem solvers along with the top executives. When they met together, what they could do became evident—their analysis of the problem, their understanding of business practices, their ability to pose variations and alternatives to discarded solutions, and so on. Even though they were well prepared for the discussions, they had to stand on their own once the session began. There was no way for the women to fake it, and there was no way for senior executives to deny their accomplishments. They saw, face to face in real time, how good these women were:

A senior VP saw some unique traits in her. He saw how she was able to focus on issues. He selected her to chair an all-male executive task force; most of the men were senior to her.

She did her job very well and got national attention. She also got a great deal of exposure to the chairman and executives outside this organization. Her performance led to a promotion where we could test her for even higher levels.

Working directly with top management also had pitfalls and ended the careers of some high-potential women. These women probably came in short of preparation or ability to respond quickly or perhaps some interpersonal qualities. A danger in direct contact at the top is that it's difficult to disguise incompetence under those circumstances. But the greater danger for high-potential women is that they will *not* have the direct contact needed to reveal their competence.

It is, of course, not possible for most up-and-coming executives to work regularly with the president and top brass on problems. Executives must find other ways to build credibility with that group. The majority of our 52 general managers developed a reputation or achieved some acclaim outside the company to complement their on-the-job accomplishments. Sometimes their outside activities and presence clearly are what allowed them to join the company or take on key assignments. Their achievements in other settings made them attractive corporate recruits.

Formal education is one area in which the general managers excelled. Forty percent had academic credentials from well-known, top-notch schools, including the most prestigious institutions. They had earned undergraduate and higher degrees from Barnard, Bryn Mawr, Columbia, Cornell, Harvard, Hunter, MIT, Smith, Stanford, Wellesley, Wharton, and Yale, among others. Some had placed very high in their class, and some had been honored with scholarships and awards.

Big-name educational credentials seemed to impress savvy insiders much as they impress the general public. The understanding is that the standards at these schools are tough, so graduation indicates the ability to achieve high standards. Also, at some of these schools, there have been only a few women competing with men. The women who have come through that experience are often recognized not only for academic rigor but also for the fortitude and flexibility needed to hold their own. Some executives described the ordeal as one in which intellectual demands were exceeded by demands on them to withstand constant isolation and rebuff by their male colleagues and professors.

This is not to say that students at other institutions less well known are not similarly challenging or noteworthy. For top management, the issue is one of reducing uncertainty about the level at which women can perform. To win academically at a big-league school is proof of one's ability. It also implies a level of sophistication and a network of useful contacts that will contribute to overall corporate performance. At other schools, particularly less well known and respected, the standards and the overall value of the educational experience are open to doubt.

Related to the source and level of education is the content—the area in which women have been educated. Some of our general managers stood out because they were trained in such traditionally male fields as math, the sciences, and computer technology. They were able to take jobs in these areas in their companies and perform at least as well as their male peers. They attracted attention because these areas were considered tough and demanding. In fact, performing well in the "hard" technical jobs, regardless of training or the lack of it, characterized a number of general managers.

Will she earn the respect of others? This is a concern of executives who must decide whether to push a woman forward in their company. A degree from Harvard, for example, is insurance of respect to many people. Advocates of high-potential women look for that, and some arrange for their protégées to get more when they can—sponsorship for an executive program at MIT or Harvard, or the best trade program available. By succeeding in these arenas, women can earn some stripes that others will recognize, even though the stripes are not from job experience per se.

Other arenas outside the company also can command corporate respect. A few of the general managers had become recognized figures on the political scene nationally, internationally, or at the statewide level. Through very high appointed positions, they achieved prominence in the government sector. Their visible savvy and other talents made them attractive candidates for corporate jobs.

Community leadership is another domain that intersects corporate life and can enhance one's credibility. Several general managers were active on local boards of directors and played key roles in the United Way campaign. In taking on these responsibilities, they worked with business leaders several levels above them, from their own company as well as from others. They interacted with senior executives as peers in some cases because of the comparable roles they held in outside governance and fund-raising activities. And more senior executives got to know them personally and see them in action. One executive remarked: "My vice president was very hard to please. Strangely enough, it was the way I ran our United Way campaign that won him over."

Being prominent in the social life of the community may also have helped some general managers get the attention of senior executives and, subsequently, a chance to take on a corporate job. Some were clearly in the right social circles and, in that realm, were peers of the top executives who create career opportunities for them. Again, the direct contact these women had with senior executives at social functions may have played a part in convincing the executives that they had marketable skills.

Perhaps the most compelling of the outside activities that the general managers took on were those related to the trade or profession. One woman was elected president of the national association in which the senior executives of her company were active, which gave her added credibility:

The company supported my being president. . . . It gave me great visibility. In that speaking role, people saw me, and I got job offers.

Often, busy people regard work outside the office as discretionary, but the backgrounds of our 52 general managers suggest that active, visible roles in the community or trade groups are important avenues for career advancement. The dilemma for many women is that while outside activity may help their career and even their morale, it still involves adding more commitments to an already overfull plate and can create more conflict in their lives. Choosing only the committees or projects that were most beneficial to them may be the strategy that the general managers used.

Extra 2: Advocacy

Women need help from above to get the kind of experience they need to be promoted, as we noted earlier. The extra of credibility makes them more fail-safe for the general management ranks; still, women probably won't break the glass ceiling without the unusually strong advocacy of a senior manager. A senior manager might spot a woman who is doing something unusual for a woman or in general. Investigation into her background might reveal some undisputable abilities. With this reasonable assurance that she is talented and able to command respect, the senior manager might give her a visible assignment in the corporation. When she performs up to par, her credibility grows and she gets another visible assignment.

Those who were willing to advocate for any of our general managers to get a visible assignment were usually those who had worked directly with them—presumably those most certain of their capabilities. Women spoke of their gratitude to a helpful boss who was special for several reasons, one often being a willingness to push them into the direct vision of senior executives. Once they were in the limelight, a higher-level executive who saw them in action sometimes picked up the ball and invited them to work directly for him or her, or placed them in yet another visible, perhaps prestigious, role in the company.

The managers and executives who advocated for these women had to believe that, despite the risk of taking an unusual and often unpopular stance in support of a woman, there was more to gain than to lose. Rosabeth Moss Kanter postulated in 1977 that executives are motivated to sponsor someone because it will gain them more power and recognition, a grateful, up-and-coming executive, and the respect of their colleagues for spotting talent and engineering the protégée's advancement for the good of the company.[2]

These gains, and possibly more, were available in the 1970s when sponsoring an executive woman. Because it was unusual to find women at high levels, the sponsor was extremely visible. If it all worked out, the sponsor could be admired as someone willing to take big risks for the company (successful ones, of course) and to stand out as an innovative, future-oriented leader. Needless to say, the sponsor's career could certainly benefit as well.

But if the potential gains were greater when a female protégée was involved, so were the risks. If the woman were to fail at center stage, her sponsor's credibility could dissolve. Instead of being seen as innovative, the sponsor could be dubbed downright loony. In addition, there might be speculation about a male sponsor's relationship with a woman who, because of her visible failure, was seen as unable to handle tough business situations. Two careers could be doomed as a result.

What kind of person would buck the odds and take the chance of advocating for an executive woman? When our executive women talked about their special bosses and senior-level sponsors, they frequently cited such qualities as being incisive, good with people, influential, politically savvy, and others that suggest their supporters were competent people themselves and well regarded in the company. In other words, they were strong managers who could afford to take the risk. If they couldn't afford an outright blemish on their track record, they could at least keep the damage to a minimum through some skillful political maneuvering. They also were influential enough to persuade others to go along with their ideas in the first place, so they had a good chance of winning an argument over whether a woman should be allowed to take on an important job.

The reasons for sponsoring a woman are not entirely clear from our study. Some executives may have backed a competent woman in a move toward social justice, unhappy that women equal to men in ability were denied the chance to contribute as fully. Other sponsors may have had different motivations for supporting a woman, but the Equal Employment Opportunity pressure probably made it easier for all of them to make a case for promoting high-potential women. Nearly 40 percent of the general managers made reference to the EEO requirements during their career that represented for them an extra in reaching their high level.

The sponsors of our general managers appear to be people who believed in the letter of the EEO law if not in the spirit of it. Judging from both the executives and the savvy insiders overall, the EEO and affirmative action pressure on these companies further reduced the risk of sponsoring a woman—*somebody* had to do it to satisfy the government, so it became a more acceptable act. If she couldn't hack it, a possible defense was that at least the government was off the company's back for a while.

Meeting the new legal requirements was a goal that many executives were working toward. We sensed, however, that a number of the executives who promoted our general managers wanted to fill the designated slots with extremely capable women who could help the company's performance in ways other than simply legal compliance. Women who were merely adequate, or worse, in visible positions would create more harm than good. In any case, a number of female executives in our study and others are convinced that, whatever their expertise or potential, they would not have gotten a chance at general management without EEO.

Extra 3: Outright Luck

One savvy insider commented that executive women, more than men, need "a break or two." Sometimes serendipity makes all the difference in a career—meeting someone who is hiring people in your field, getting into a business that is on the up-swing, and playing a role in a project that attracts national at-tention are all examples of how luck and timing can help your career. Naturally, luck and ability are often related. Getting a boss who is willing to promote a woman, being a young profes-sional when the Equal Employment Opportunity Commission pushed strongly for women in management, or being the only one around at the time who knows something about a problem are all examples of how luck can join with ability to help some-one succeed.

One break that 13 of our 52 general managers mentioned was a reorganization of the company that opened some career opportunities to them. Some got to play an active role in the merger or divestiture itself—the process of reorganization was the forum for them to take on new responsibilities, work with top executives, or represent the company. For others, an acqui-sition created new testing grounds that they entered and in which they proved themselves.

Deregulation of whole industries forced reorganization in a number of companies to cope with the change in products or services to be supplied. The financial services industry is one represented in our study that went through a traumatic transi-tion in the late 1970s when restrictions were lifted and compa-nies began to compete for customers. In the frenzied attempt to shape business to the changed environment, new units that had to be managed were created. Women were given some of these new positions—because they were immediately available, or they had a lengthy service record, or they were believed to be well suited to functions such as customer service that had be-come critical to survival. For whatever reason, women got a ca-reer boost via the restructuring of the industry.

Mergermania also gave women chances to move ahead in their career. The shake-up of large companies going through a merger created opportunities—as executives quit or were forced out, openings were sometimes filled by women who may have been considered loyal lieutenants to the top executives. Some general managers made reference to these reorganizations as playing a part in their career progress. Others from the same company or the same industry didn't mention such situations in our interview, but they may have been affected by them as well.

The career opportunities created by reorganizations are not unique to women. In our study of male executives, savvy insiders cited reorganizations as a factor that contributed to the success (and the derailment) of high-potential male executives. Whether they play a bigger part in the success of female executives is not clear. One hypothesis is that in the chaos of a reorganization, a woman can slip into a previously off-limits job while senior executives are distracted by other issues. Since few key jobs are off-limits to men, reorganization may be a unique advantage to women in breaking the glass ceiling.

Luck and timing work to the good of aspiring executives, but they also work to their detriment. Some women were said to have derailed once a reorganization took place, and some of our general managers recounted the career setbacks they had as a result of a reorganization. Women succumb to the whims of fate just as men do. If there is a difference between women and men, it may be that women need more luck (along with more ability) to get ahead because of the barriers they confront. Even good luck can be hazardous to a woman's career, however, because many people are more than willing to attribute her progress or achievements to luck and not to her capabilities.

Two researchers from the University of Texas at Arlington, Howard Garland and Kenneth Price, in examining a number of studies on perceptions of why people succeed, found that people attribute the above-average performance of a man more to his skill than to luck. However, the same level of performance by a woman is attributed more to luck than to her abilities. These authors conclude:

An individual could maintain a strong bias against women in management in the face of information about a successful female manager by attributing her success to some external cause . . . the female manager is not given personal credit for her success.[3]

Another example of luck being used to explain the success of women is the story of Katharine Graham. Many people know that, for more than twenty years, since 1963, she was the only female CEO of a Fortune 500 company. Many people also know that she took control of the *Washington Post* after her husband's death, as *Forbes* and other publications are quick to reveal in their reports.[4] In other words, she inherited the reins of power from her husband, which casts some doubt on her ability. We are left with the question, Without that marriage and her husband's untimely death, could she have reached that level? Was she just lucky?

What most people *don't* know about the *Washington Post* situation is that Katharine's father bought that business in 1933, and he chose her husband, Philip Graham, to run the family affairs. Philip had as much of an advantage via family connections as did Katharine. He was just as "lucky," but few people mention it or are particularly bothered by it. Probably a fair number of male CEOs of large companies had family connections or other forms of luck, but perhaps we hear less about them because people tend to attribute men's success to their own skills.

Executive women do need some luck to break the glass ceiling, but luck alone does not work. Luck in combination with competence and support makes this milestone possible. These three extras are not always within one's control, but they may make the difference between women who have succeeded to general managment and those who still see the glass ceiling above them.

Hitting the Wall
Facing Limits, Finding Alternatives

CHAPTER 7

There is corporate support [of women] for a time; but when you get close, barriers are put up. The criteria are different for women and men. The doors aren't really wide open. It's scary for this company right now—we have some senior [female] line managers.

The women they hire here are different from the men. They (top management) don't want any women who are a threat to them. I don't think there will be any women VPs at this company in my lifetime. But even if there is—ultimately one woman always gets through—the problem is that 99 percent don't.

What's next for me? I could take a lateral move. Or I could have my boss's job, which I don't want—not with a three-year-old, anyway; maybe later. I don't want a business job, and they probably wouldn't offer me one. I wouldn't go someplace else and have to prove myself again. . . . My future is unlimited. I could quit tomorrow if I wanted to. I've worked for so long I don't know what I want. I don't have many interests outside work, but now that I've gotten a handle on my job, I have to think about what I want next. I'm at a crossroads.

Once they had beaten the odds and broken through the glass ceiling into general management, most of the women in our study stopped short. They looked ahead to senior management and saw another barrier. Instead of a transparent glass ceiling above them, these women now found a wall in front of them of extremely sturdy construction.

139

When we asked a question about the future—"Where do you see your career moving? What's next for you?"—more than two-thirds of the general managers acknowledged that there were limits on how much farther they could move. Some thought they could go one level higher before plateauing, some expected not to go any higher, and a few were unsure and wouldn't venture a guess. The reasons for curbing their careers were varied. Having too narrow a business base, aging out, discrimination, and family conflicts were cited frequently as barriers, although some said that any limits on their career were a result of their own actions.

One-third of the executives were more optimistic:

It's still very open-ended. There are two possibilities, probably in the next couple of months—a move up in human resources or a line job. My dream is executive management, to be in the core of fifty managers where my boss is. I don't care if I'm the first woman. I think a woman will be there within the next year or two. Maybe it will be me a couple of years from now. There are no limits unless I decide to put them on. Even if I have children, there are ways to combine things.

Even some of these executives, though, called attention to limits on how high they could go. Some in staff jobs saw a switch to line as unlikely. Several dismissed the notion of going as high as president or CEO because they weren't qualified, because of their gender, or because they didn't want to. Sometimes they insisted that the choice was their own and not really a limit:

It's unlikely that I'll be CEO. . . . Anyway, as I look for more balance, I'm not sure I aspire to a CEO position. The sacrifices are greater than I want to make.

For most of the general managers, continuing the rather single-minded upward climb is a pursuit they appear to be abandoning. Only 3 of our executives said they thought they could be president or CEO of their company. For most of the rest, the rewards seemed not worth the risks. Most are convinced that they would have received more rewards already if they were men, and now they face the strong possibility that the risk/reward ratio will be even worse. The odds against them are much larger than those they faced at each preceding level. The corporate pyramid grows so narrow at the top for everyone that it is unlikely they will survive the competition, let alone the perceived discrimination. No, many are saying, that kind of success is not worth it.

We predict that no more than a handful of our 76 executives will enter that topmost core of executives called senior management, and none of those will reach as high as the presidency of their corporation. The vast majority will derail (if they haven't plateaued already) because of the obstacles in their path, or they will reject the option of moving into that echelon for one reason or another.

This prediction is hardly devastating to many women who participated in our research and others who are at or near the general management level. Some women enjoy being one of the top three hundred or five hundred managers in a company that may have fifty thousand employees. Their work is challenging, they influence major decisions, they make gobs of money and live the good life. They have what they want in the way of corporate responsibility. Besides, some must reason, why lust after something that is off-limits? It's not such a bad deal to stay, or it could be just the kind of credible track record needed to do well in an entrepreneurial venture.

Many women will feel only moderate pain at having to withdraw as a serious candidate for the top. But the damage done by limiting the field to men only is greater than simply the psychological impact on some pretty special individuals. A whole cadre of potentially excellent senior executives is being passed over. In limiting the contributions that women executives can make, the human resources available to corporations are not being used effectively.

Can business still afford to pass up the talent available in the pool of women who have or could manage substantial assets and missions? Why aren't shareholders screaming bloody murder at the wastefulness their companies are displaying? Why isn't top management eager to work side by side with extremely talented women and to turn them loose with large pieces of the corporate pie? Why do so many of the women who have committed and achieved more than their male colleagues seem to be abandoned when the stakes reach a certain level?

Through our research, we have found that there are three main barriers keeping female executives out of the inner sanctum of senior management. These barriers are similar to those that plague women at other management levels, so they are familiar to these executives. In some cases, the barriers may be experienced much the same as they were before; in others, they may be more intense. For everyone, they are more disconcerting at this point because the women believe they have already paid their dues. After breaking the glass ceiling, many women realize that they are still not on the road to the top, that they are hemmed in even more than they were, and that the support that was so helpful in the past all of a sudden becomes scarce.

No Road to the Top

When I came, there were two women with the corporation [in management], and they were a joke. Both were acquired during an acquisition.

Women who rose in the same era as some of our 76 executives were considered out-of-place in the business world, according to some savvy insiders. From the stories the executives told, women were often the butt of jokes, pranks, and outright malice. Many gained entry by virtue of their staff roles as analysts or attorneys or accountants, tolerated as specialists in dead-end pockets of the company. When they made it clear that they wanted to be full-fledged members of the executive team, they were sometimes ridiculed or sabotaged. Neither they nor anyone else who may have wanted to help them really knew how to overcome this obstacle, since it had never been done.

Certain staff roles were important enough to warrant a spot on the management committee, and if they and their advocates made enough of an issue of it, sometimes women were awarded those spots. This was the only road available to women, unless they fought for jobs considered to be in the business mainstream, where there were legitimate routes to the top—routes that had been taken by past CEOs and presidents of the company. These were the routes that young men considered to have potential to be the next leaders of the corporation were nudged into by their sponsors. These are the routes being taken now by some of the executives in our study, and quite a few more spoke wistfully of getting such a chance to broaden their experience so that they would be considered for the most senior jobs in the company:

Within the next two years, I face a tough choice. There's an easy career ladder now to group vice president, on the staff side. There are no competitors. Should I make a lateral move to the line side? It would delay a vice president position a couple of years. My job now is about five times bigger than I am. I'm still learning. I need to think this through. If I stay on the staff side, I cannot become one of the top few executives in [this company]. But I'd have lots of power. . . .

Unlike their fast-track male counterparts who rotate through staff positions or rise in visible and important staff positions in finance or law, few women get the chance to throw off the stigma of being "staff." Even the most talented women, after rising through a series of increasingly complex staff roles, are sometimes viewed as having a "staff mentality" and dismissed as serious contenders for higher levels. But some have gotten or will get their chance too late to be a serious contender for president, or even one or two levels below. The savvy insiders agreed, as much as they agreed on anything, that line jobs are necessary to make senior management potential a reality for women. *Any* line job was closed to women, some said, until recently—now women are admitted, even recruited, into line jobs, and some see that as the solution to getting women to the top:

A staff job was the past road to the top [for women]. Now we're more willing to put women into line jobs. We have more women to pick from than before. There will be far more women in top executive jobs in the next ten years. The availability of women and the acceptance level are increasing. Everyone is getting smarter about matching talent with job specifications. People in staff get only so high. The road to the top is characterized by the most aggressive. More women now understand what is required, and we understand what we're looking for.

But the outlook was not universally positive among the savvy insiders. In fact, most of them pointed out the progress that is *not* being made. Some contended that line jobs remain barred to women. The parts of the company most likely to produce top female executives are still the staff areas, they argued, because that is where women have made achievements and it is the only area in which women are accepted.

Even when women can grab the golden ring and get a line job, it is more likely to be a job that is not in a crucial part of the business. On top of that, the women we interviewed do not get the kind of experience in line jobs that can mark them as leaders—turning around a floundering business unit or starting new product lines, for example. One of our general managers said that her continued progress would be hampered because she would not get the overseas assignments she needed. The men we studied earlier had more start-up assignments and trouble-shooting roles that broadened their experience and helped establish their credibility. These line-oriented challenges seem to be off-limits to women in many companies. One woman who attended a presentation on this project commented that women still get assigned to fix morale problems rather than problems that are more directly measurable.

At this point, neither the staff nor the line side is the road to the top for women. Women have been stereotyped as "staff people"; more important, they have not attained the powerful positions either in staff or in line to prove themselves. And finally, they still lack the assignments and experience that produce the kinds of managers who are tapped for the top jobs.

Because they have seen one or two women get to a remarkably high level, executives are tempted to say there is now a road to the top. From our vantage point, that road is an illusion.

Hemmed In

Many of the pioneer women in our study felt terribly confined. They had to avoid being feminine *and* avoid being macho. They had to get the right kinds of help *and* succeed on their own. They had to take risks without making mistakes. They had to keep the home fires burning while they made their career. Thank goodness, some executives sighed, women have more freedom and flexibility now. They talked about their hatred of the "uniform"—a tailored dark suit with a silk tie—and the joy of wearing a dress instead. They talked about having a baby without the additional burden of taking on a husband. They talked about not being afraid to manage in whatever style suited them.

Are there fewer restrictions today, as some claim, on how executives dress, behave, and perform? Or is the band of acceptability narrower and more restrictive for women at the top level of management? Although some of the norms are changing, our assessment is that expectations of women increase even more at higher levels. Top jobs are so restrictive, in fact, that most women don't stand a chance.

Executive women continue to be hemmed in by the multiple and conflicting expectations that have plagued them at every level. In addition, the myth of "feminine leadership" is still alive and well in senior management. It may be that in the past, women had to have a more-like-a-man-than-men aura, but now women may be caught up in the expectation that using a feminine style can create organizational change. When top executive men start to believe that women manage differently from men, and they bring a woman into a job expecting her to perform business miracles through a uniquely "feminine style," the proverbial cookie crumbles.

More important, when candidates are being considered for senior management positions, the criteria, restrictions, and expectations become subtle and subjective for everyone, both men and women. Since all of the candidates tend to be top performers, chemistry plays a major part in who advances and who doesn't. Women are different and, by definition, outsiders. Accentuating those differences, whether real or imagined, serves to fortify rather than destroy barriers to the top. When looking for someone to run a failing business, senior executives may overlook an otherwise suitable candidate because they assume that her feminine leadership style will doom her to fail.

A Vanishing Support System

The executives we interviewed had been barraged with lack of acceptance of their careers. Some of the older women pointed out that for a married woman with children to go to work when they did was unthinkable. Going to college was against tradition for some, and others were considered freakish for studying anything but home economics. There was no shortage of corporate club members to tell them, in various ways, how unwelcome they were.

Sometimes their bosses had told them outright that they shouldn't have their job. Some of their colleagues had networked around them as if they didn't exist. Their families had sometimes demanded that the domestic traditions also be maintained. They had no time for friendships.

Although operating in a generally unsupportive environment, these executives did get crucial help along the way, and they took advantage of it. As we noted in earlier chapters, help from above often made the difference in the advancement of the executives in our study. In many cases, this kind of help allowed women to break the glass ceiling. Once they achieved the general management level, however, some executives found that their support system had become precarious.

Although it is risky to sponsor a woman for general management, some senior executives are willing to take the chance because their career is enhanced if the woman proves successful. At more senior levels, hardly anyone is willing to take this kind of risk. One reason may be that women, once promoted to peer levels, become competitors for the few top jobs available. Or mistakes in selection, if the woman chosen performs poorly, will reflect on the male executive's reputation, revealing him to be a sorry judge of talent.

In addition, these women are no longer getting help from EEO. First, as we inferred earlier, the teeth are gone from the legislation because the Reagan administration is not enforcing EEO. On top of that, EEO never did have much impact at senior levels of a company.

Meanwhile, at home, the pressures and expectations remain the same, plus a new element often makes this environment also unsupporting. Many women at the general management level earn more than their husbands and have moved faster in their careers. These facts can create conflict, and formerly supportive husbands sometimes turn hostile.

Many executive women, then, now stand alone in a new corporate environment where the rules have changed once again. Their former sponsors may have become competitors, the road to moving ahead may not be clear, and there may be new conflicts at home.

The Final Straw—Exhaustion

Although many female executives face these three new barriers to their advancement, ways could probably be found to deal with them—if it weren't for a new factor that at this stage cripples the ability of many to move ahead. Their resources have run dry, and these women are exhausted. We think this has happened to a number of our 76 executives.

A few don't want to move up because the responsibilities at higher levels are less attractive than what they're doing now—more policing than making operating decisions, for example. But many who claimed not to want a top job saw the demands at higher levels as too stifling, even overpowering:

Now I question moving up even to [the next level]. I ask myself, Do I want to commit more of my life to my job? I don't know. I guess I'm not hungry enough. The train is moving a little fast for me now. I might be happier moving slower, at least for a while.

Some of these general managers were on a fast track that moved them into a new job before they had time to be relatively good at the preceding job, so they always felt frustrated and somewhat inept. One executive expressed her discontent in answering the question, "What's next for you?"

Beats me. I'm overwhelmed and overworked. Most of us are. I'd like to work for a smaller organization, but I have no plans to leave.

Staying in the same job, having the time to work things into shape and become really good at it, was a goal of a number of general managers. They felt they had lost something by moving and they wanted a breather, even if it took five years in the same job to feel they had mastered it along with the rest of their life.

Clearly, a number of our general managers felt they had been running a rat race to progress in their company. Most believed that their upward progress was nearly over. A remarkable level of ambivalence and ambiguity was reflected in what they said about their career status. We have to wonder whether the majority, who see a wall before them, have subconsciously thrown in the towel, focusing on the chance to turn their energies elsewhere instead of grieving over an aborted career. Have they decided not to want what is not available? Are they afraid to admit they have been stumped? Are they tired of waging war against the corporate system?

Most female executives have been dealing with ambiguity throughout their professional lives, as the first woman to do this or that in the company. Their experience has no doubt equipped them to cope better with the current situation. In the process, however, they have learned that to fight for the jobs they want is painful and that to consistently demonstrate their competence to the satisfaction of others is consuming. They now have a good idea of the energy required and of what they must leave by the wayside as they tackle an executive job.

These executives are savvy. But many are also tired and a bit fed up with the extraordinary expectations that others have of them. They would like to drop the endless struggle, but they have a tough time doing so. At fifty years old, one executive feels she is as high as she can go in the company. She wants to start a catering business with her husband, something fun and rewarding that would give her time to herself.

I did my dream. I don't need to do more to satisfy myself. I wanted to compete and do a lot of firsts. That drove me back into the work force. I've done firsts, and I've gotten recognition for those.

But even she doesn't completely believe that. Maybe, she later added, if the opportunity arose to head a certain department, "I might just take it. It would be another first." Clearly, opting out is not an easy decision to make, but some executives are resigning themselves to it.

The Alternatives

Myra Strober of Stanford University summed it up in a 1984 *Fortune* article: "The problem of the 1970s was bringing women into the corporation. The problem of the 1980s is keeping them there."[1]

Women managers are starting to leave companies at an alarming rate. A study reported in a 1986 *Fortune* cover story said that one out of every four women managers is leaving America's companies.[2] As we noted, they leave because they are exhausted and fed up with the unrealistic expectations constantly placed on them in the corporate environment. But they also leave because there are positive alternatives for them.

Some executives in our study dreamed of leaving the corporate life and finding a better way of living:

I don't want to be the first female president or CEO of [this company]. I don't have the stamina for that. I'm honest about that now with myself. I want to retire at fifty-five and start a second business—something different, like a frame factory. I like art—I like to see what people are putting up. I'd be able to putz around, be my own boss, have people contact. My husband and I could do that together. It could be a real partnership. That's one thing that appeals to me about it.

The good life that executives dream about is often outside corporate life. Even if they believe they can still go higher in their company, a number of executives dream about making a go of it in a radically different arena. Fifteen have the idea of running their own business on their mind, anything from consulting in the same field to landscaping or catering, sometimes in conjunction with a friend or relative. Five executives said they dream about entering politics, aiming as high as a cabinet position or state governor. Others want to sing or dance or play an instrument, or to go back to school for a Ph.D., or to run a university or a foundation, or to be a motivational speaker.

It may be reasonable to expect dreams to be different from reality. After all, isn't that what makes them dreams? But that only 12 of 74 executives said their dream involved having a senior management role in their company may be significant. One general manager said she might just as soon take early retirement so she can "read and do science things" as be promoted into one of the top ten jobs in her company. A number of executives are torn between working and—in the larger sense—living. They want to have children, spend time with their husband, support their parents, build friendships, and do other things that they postponed to reach the level they did.

Other researchers also have found that female executives would often rather be somewhere else, and that large numbers are in fact leaving their company to start a business of their own. According to the *Wall Street Journal*, the 1985 Bureau of Labor Statistics lists 2.8 million self-employed women in the United States, a 43 percent leap from a decade earlier.[3] Some of these women deserted the corporate climb, despite the potential they showed there. A follow-up survey of the "73 Women Ready to Run Corporate America" found that, only a year later, 10 percent had taken a "new route around the glass ceiling: they've become entrepreneurs."[4]

Judging from the remarks of our executives, and others, their turning to entrepreneurship is related to the pain and difficulty of being in the corporate world as much as to the appeal of heading one's own firm or enjoying a hobby long put on the back burner. One manager interviewed by *Fortune* who left her company said, "I was told I wouldn't make it into senior management at my bank. Maybe I just didn't have it. But the bank never found any woman who did. They were operating under a consent decree and they brought in a lot of women at the vice president level. Every single one of them left."[5] The push factor, in other words, is as great as the elements that pull them into something new. There is the felt need, sometimes disguised, for executive women just to get the hell out.

A few of the male executives also expressed some concern over the work versus life dilemma, feeling a need to assess their own values and set priorities. When they were asked about what's next, 9 talked about doing something different, mostly retirement (even if it was ten and a half years down the road!). A few of them were in a dilemma, trying to sort out what they really wanted and how much they would pay:

I just turned forty, and I'm reviewing. Am I satisfied? I'm looking at options.

I have a different problem right now—Is the game worth the candle? . . . Do I want to continue doing this type of work?

When we asked the women about their future, considerably more (31) reported wanting to do something radically different even if they felt they could still progress in their company. As we've noted, these include running a business, holding political office, becoming a lobbyist, or obtaining a Ph.D.

Most of the men, however, were not abandoning the climb or feeling stymied. Most gave some indication that they believed they were still moving up. Yet the majority of our 76 executive women, even those who had already entered general management, appeared to feel out of the running for senior management jobs in their companies. Perhaps some were too pessimistic about their chances of being tapped for the corporation presidency or a key job reporting directly to the president;

a few may end up getting an offer they didn't expect. But per-haps some of those who saw no limits on their career potential will be in for a surprise as well—a rather nasty surprise—when they discover that their superiors don't share their optimism.

We predict that the majority of the 76 female executives in our study will opt out. Some will be part of the corporate exo-dus, leaving to run their own show. Some will lighten the career demands so that they can have the family life they want. Some will simply run out of steam. They will leave the fight for ad-vancement to those who follow in their footsteps.

The commitment required to handle top jobs is great for anyone, female or male. But we believe that the dilemma is more powerful for women because of the three levels of pres-sure we identified in chapter 1. Although both sexes must en-dure heavy job demands, female executives must serve more as symbols and role models. They also must endure on-the-job pregnancy, the vagaries of child care, and child-rearing, know-ing that trying to combine a family and a career might get them deleted from the list for top jobs.

One CEO we interviewed was frustrated, perceiving that women expected to have the same chances and rewards as men, while quitting even senior management jobs to have or be with their family. Women haven't yet made the commitment, he ar-gued. Many men in senior management say the same things behind closed doors. We fear that this may lead to a new kind of discrimination—that instead of companies finding ways to keep women, they will have a new excuse to slow down or stop their advancement.

In reality, women must choose to give up a great deal for a shot not at the top job, but maybe at one of the top fifty jobs in the company. Few savvy insiders or executive women we inter-viewed expected to see a woman head their company in their lifetime. Women face a different choice, and the commitment should be in line with the payoff. It is evident to some extent

that executives control what they can control—their commitment to the corporate climb—as they start to realize that the
payoff is not as great as they had hoped. They confront the goals
they have had perhaps all their lives, and some feel forced to
put them to rest.

The Future
Can Women Make It to the Top?

CHAPTER 8

Although I thoroughly enjoy the success I have achieved, I am dismayed that so few other women can claim to be making it in the business world. For years, I have felt that it would be my generation that would bring true equality for men and women to the workplace. Contrarily, I find the 1980s to be a dangerous and precarious period because corporate and government leaders are beginning to perceive that an investment in the training and leadership development of women is unlikely to yield the same return as an equivalent investment in men.

In a 1986 speech she gave to the New York Financial Women's Association, Jane Evans, managing partner of Montgomery Securities, outlined succinctly the new dangers that executive women face today.[1]

By their own admission, most of the executive women in our study will not enter the inner sanctum of senior management in their company, let alone head it as the CEO. In fact, a 1984 *Fortune* article declared that *no* woman currently is on the fast track to the top.[2]

But the story doesn't end with these executives. They are called pioneers because they are followed by other women who are swarming into professional and management roles with their sights set on senior management and their expectations heightened by seeing others break through the glass ceiling.

Some people have argued that the "old guard," who became the first and only women within their respective corporate

155

domains, experienced life so differently from their successors that they can't be compared meaningfully. The environment is so different now, the argument goes, that with the influx into middle management of women who have the "right background" many will eventually ascend into senior management. Many people, including some of the 76 executives in our study, believe that the potential for top jobs of women now in the pipeline is dramatically better than the slim potential of the pioneers as a group.

Three factors are cited repeatedly in the popular press to show the changing corporate environment and how those changes will help women in the future. The fundamental theory is that it is "only a matter of time" before a new generation of women not only breaks the glass ceiling but also crashes right through the wall to the top. This theory is supported by the idea that since a whole generation of older, more traditional male leaders will retire soon, younger men will be more supportive of female executives. In addition, the next generation of women has terrific role models to emulate in the pioneers who fought their way to the general management level, easing the way for all who follow. As we have studied our research as well as the work of others, we have come to the conclusion that, unfortunately, these factors are more myth than reality.

It's Only a Matter of Time

A somewhat gilded picture of the corporate climb is held by a number of young women in the early stages of their careers, women who feel very distant from their predecessors, according to a March 1986 *Working Woman* article, "The New Shoot-out at Generation Gap."[3] These younger women had a much easier time getting into the right schools, into the right fields, and onto the right management track. They don't understand what the fuss is all about, nor why the pioneer women at higher levels have to be so suspicious and uptight.

Their balloon bursts within a few years, according to some who have been there. In an interview for *Business Week* in 1984, an engineer commented, "It's not till you get into your fifth or sixth year that you suddenly start realizing that men with half of your ability are passing you by."[4] Some more experienced women see that younger women have been seduced into thinking that they have been fully accepted into the business world and that they will be treated equally.

A woman who recently phoned one of us was clearly angry that some people had such a naive, destructive belief. She told a story about how her friend, an executive woman who confided in her periodically, had become exasperated recently over an incident with a younger woman in the engineering company she worked for. "I don't know what I'll do if I have to face another thirty-two-year old engineer who comes to my office in tears," she lamented. "These young women have moved ahead—they haven't felt that they were victims of discrimination. Then they are devastated when they encounter someone through their work who hates their guts simply because they are women. They think that will never happen to them," she explained, "and when it does, they don't know how to deal with it."

The statistics hold plenty of evidence that women have an easier, faster start on their career now than they did in the past. The problem is that getting women *into* corporations is not the same as moving them *up*. The top management ranks of large corporations still seem to be nearly as forbidden to women as ever. In fact, we conclude that senior management will be off-limits to women now in the management pipeline—women in their twenties—to about the same extent as it is to executive women today. We expect to see no more than a handful of women reach the senior management level of Fortune 100-sized corporations within the next two decades, because the barriers that keep women out of senior management today will remain.

Change takes time—decades—and the kind of change we view as necessary involves change in institutions, change in attitudes, and change in behavior. To say that there may now exist the beginnings of a road to the top is not enough. Women must experience the broad range of activities that help prepare them to run a business. No one, woman or man, can be a "thirty-day wonder" and attain success as CEO of a Fortune 100 corporation. John Kotter points out that it takes twenty years to develop a general manager.[5] It has been a little over ten years since the first woman graduated from the Harvard Business School, and only in the last few years have women obtained the kinds of experience that may be helpful in their development.

One of the pioneer women we interviewed said optimistically about the future:

We've made scads of progress. There are more women in the organization to draw on, and the culture accepts women now. As even more women come in, even more assimilation will occur. My theory is that time will heal all wounds.

Then she added:

But I recently said this to a young woman at lunch, and she replied, "Yes, but I'll be dead by then."

Attitudes change slowly, and women will be subjected to sex stereotypes for a long time to come. The *Harvard Business Review* 1985 study of nearly 800 male and female executives showed some substantial differences from the earlier survey in 1965 in readers' perceptions of women in management, but the authors reported that the news "is not all that good. Almost half the women surveyed still believe women will never be completely accepted as executives in corporate America."[6]

If such attitudes persist, they must be countered for women to progress. Yet one countervailing force, formal Equal Employment Opportunity pressure, has been diminished and may not be an effective factor in the future if the administration doesn't turn around. Most of the *HBR* 1985 respondents believed that EEO has had a positive impact on the careers of women. One respondent noted that "women in management have made tremendous advances over the last ten years, which I believe reflects the excellence and competence of those women who have succeeded. However, sad to say, I do not believe many of those opportunities would have arisen in the first place without equal opportunity legislation and oversight by federal and local governments."[7]

Without enforcement, the question is whether young women in business will receive the assignments and promotions they'll need to compete along the way for top jobs. They may know better than their predecessors the importance of mainstream jobs, overseas stints, and other stripes they'll need to put on their sleeves, but their access to them could still be very limited without the government actively supporting them.

Women also may be increasingly hemmed in by the trend toward "lean, mean" organizational structures. Basia Hellwig reported in 1985 that 53 percent of the "73 Women Ready to Run Corporate America" believe career progress will be harder as structural change in organizations creates more competition for fewer top jobs.[8] Some of the women we interviewed saw this trend in their own companies:

There are now lots of people at my level, so new challenges may be limited. The pyramid begins to get narrow from here on. I'll face some new competition within four to five years. It will be a real point of decision for me—stay or go. I don't know what I'll do.

According to the September 9, 1986, issue of the *Wall Street Journal*, we are already seeing "the ax fall increasingly on top management women. . . . Where corporations may have delayed firing women in the past, now the kid gloves have been taken off."[9] The massive restructuring of American industry that is taking place may become the perfect excuse for no longer supporting the advancement of women, or any other minority.

Younger Men Will Be More Supportive

The support system in general for women coming along the track has its thin spots. One weak point continues to be male colleagues and higher-level executives. One theory holds that the older generation of men who held women back is now retiring en masse, and their replacements—younger men in their forties and fifties—are more accustomed to working with women and thus more accepting of them as peers and direct reports. But there may be a glitch, as one savvy insider explained:

The road is more open now, but the very top will take another generation for top management to feel comfortable with women. They didn't rub shoulders with women in school. But men now realize that women are more aggressive [about getting] jobs, so maybe they're not as willing to be supportive.

At least some of the older top executives who lent their hand to women on the way up the ladder probably were inspired by a fatherly (or grandfatherly) perspective—safe, distant, and in some ways, naive about career women. But the modern men ascending the corporate pyramid are more familiar with women in business, and at least some regard them as threatening competition. In fact, the 1985 *HBR* survey data showed a *less* favorable attitude among younger men. The authors explained:

Many young men are undoubtedly competing with women for promotions. Understandably, such competition may create animosity toward their female counterparts and color their opinions of female executives in general.[10]

Others concur that there is more competition now for fewer jobs up the corporate ladder. Roughly half of the corporate recruiters and executive women interviewed in the 1985 *Working Woman* study said that progress for women will be harder, not easier, because of this. The changing of the guard may not be a purely positive change for women, as some have proclaimed.

Balancing home and career is another problem that many women need support to handle, and today the system still lets them down. A few executives remarked that women have an easier time of it now because their husbands (or male companions) share the household management. Frankly, we didn't see much evidence that this social phenomenon is occurring. Some of the young executives we interviewed were frustrated by the unwillingness of their husbands to carry their share of the household load. The men's gestures to "help" with the groceries or cleaning hardly make a dent in the work and reinforce the notion that it is *her* job to do it all.

Because women are pursuing a career earlier than women did before and not waiting until their children are grown, some of our executives were concerned that the pressure on women is even greater now:

There is a big trade-off for women today—they have to deal with the dual-career situation sooner.

The constant juggle is likely to create problems at the office and at home for executive women still in their thirties. Dual-career marriage problems also affect younger men who represent the new guard in the executive suite, and such problems may help explain why younger men are not very supportive of executive women. The *HBR* authors speculated that some men "may transfer some of their hostility to other working women."[11] The responsibilities women still bear for home and hearth take their toll not only on them, but also on their husbands, who then may take out their resentment on female colleagues at work, and so on.

They Have Strong Role Models

Younger women do have a source of support that wasn't available in the old days—other women at higher levels (at least a few, assuming some stay). Will that make a significant difference in their support system and therefore represent a major advantage? "Absolutely!" is what some executives said. Others see it as a definite disadvantage.

The advantages, of course, are ones that the women we interviewed said they missed so much—of having the trail blazed ahead of them, and a role model or two for guidance and a helping hand. The disadvantage is less obvious. The fact is, the pioneer women, who are counted on as role models and mentors for younger women, often are not able to perform these roles as expected because of the intense and constant pressures on them to be good team players and consistently outstanding performers.

The inability of top-level women to coach and advocate for other women in the company causes great concern in several camps—the younger women, who still need help; the senior executive men, who are still unsure around women and who may be expecting executive women to take over the developmental reins; and the executives themselves, who frequently see themselves as social change agents yet are limited in what they can contribute to the cause.

Executive women are limited because their plate is already full of obligations. Many are stretched thin, meeting all the demands on them already, so they can do only so much to help others advance their career. A number of them *are* responsive to other women not as far along in their careers—they give advice (or just listen), and they push for promotions and key assignments. A few have started support groups for women within their company. But if they put much energy into helping others, they risk not having enough left to promote their own career and have a personal life.

Most of the women we interviewed (61 percent) said they don't try to be a role model. Their comments reveal that most of the women who feel they are a role model just by virtue of their position don't think much about it or don't know how to handle the responsibility they feel it imposes upon them. They accept that role reluctantly—they are trying to protect themselves from yet another source of pressure. The conflict is troublesome to them, because they know how valuable they could be to other women and they believe in "the cause." But they also know that their own success is fragile, and if they fail in their own endeavors, that will hurt other women at least as much as will their not giving them counsel and visibility. They have to find another happy medium, one that constitutes doing enough for other women while also looking out for themselves—an additional juggling act that they are not eager to take on.

Their energy and time are not the only resources executive women must protect in accepting some responsibility for other women. They also feel pressure to develop both men and women so that they can assign and reward their people on a basis that is "fair" rather than chauvinistic. In other words, they are determined to avoid being guilty of the same thing that men were to limit their prospects—sexism. They also feel some pressure to be a corporate team player, to fit in, and to do what's best for the company by developing talent wherever it lies, whether in women or men.

These executives can't afford to be seen as separatists who surround themselves only with other women, not after they have invested so much in eliminating differences related solely to gender. So again they are torn, looking for ways to gain the support of their subordinates and their superiors. In the process, some of the younger women who were counting on their help are left to fend for themselves.

In our interviews, we detected a genuine desire in executives to help other women coming along, not to hurt them. They want to see the world become a better place for women, but they sometimes feel limited in what they can do to help without risking more themselves. One way to cope with such a painful dilemma is to remove the problem psychologically, to take the position that it is no longer difficult for women to get ahead, that discrimination is a thing of the past. Psychologist Janet Spence once called this a kind of hysterical blindness that women sometimes use as a coping mechanism. When she hears a woman say about the prognosis for women in business that "there is no problem," she often suspects that the woman is protecting herself.

The "see no evil" syndrome may be at work in many companies. It is a natural, even logical, reaction to a situation in which executive women feel that certain key advantages are being taken away and yet even more is expected of them. Not only are they no longer the "curiosity" that got them access to people, but they also feel responsible for helping other women along. The syndrome works for men, too, who are tired of the pressure and baffled by how to solve the problem of giving women equal opportunity in the executive suite. Others who "see no evil" may simply have stopped looking for any signs to the contrary.

The Wheels of Progress *Are* Turning

We are not trying to paint a universally bleak picture. We do think it is important to have a clear-eyed view of the situation, however. Without that, determining the best way of moving forward will be difficult.

While the world has not changed so much that the twenty-five-year-old woman with her heart set on becoming the CEO of a Fortune 100 company is likely to be satisfied, we do believe she stands a much greater chance of getting into general management than did her predecessors. Although the road to the top is not clear and not straight, the path to the general management level is better marked. We think that as long as the momentum for advancement is maintained, the next generation will have a far easier chance to become general managers. Because the climb is easier, they may have more energy to attack the remaining barriers to top management. A handful of women have made it to the top in Fortune 500-sized companies; maybe in another generation or so, a like number will break down the wall in Fortune 100-sized companies.

This is not the ideal scenario, since many who want to see women in top posts will probably not live to do so. In the meantime, we must try to content ourselves with the gains that are made and the comfort of knowing that the ascent of women into top management, although slower than we'd like, *is* inevitable if the concerted effort to keep the momentum going continues. Fortunately, there seem to be enough interested parties willing and able to push for the changes needed to assure continued progress; we predict that women will take top management posts within the next fifty years.

The problem has no easy answers or quick fixes. No blueprint can be laid out for handling an issue so full of complexities: economic, cultural, psychological, sociological. What we do know is that keeping the momentum going on as many fronts as possible is crucial.

What Companies Are Doing

In some large corporations, the pressures on executive women are being decreased via a number of programs and services. The kinds of help that our 76 executives said they needed are being built into the system, and they will help the future generations increase the odds of surviving and thriving at the highest corporate levels.

There appears to be a growing realization that women can't become men. Despite the similarities in their abilities, motives, and styles that are being more widely recognized, some differences still create barriers for women. Simply being a woman in a man's world is one major difference. (Blacks and other minorities, of course, must also face the same issue.) Also, being the one who must carry and deliver the children is another career barrier that is exclusive to women. These peculiar factors are emerging as issues with which the company at large must deal. Finally, some have come around to the stance that Harvard professor Rosabeth Moss Kanter, in her 1986 article "Mastering Change: The Skills We Need," recently described: "I wonder whether there has been too much emphasis on teaching women to conform, to fit into the system. Certainly that suits conservative organizations in conservative times. But now . . . innovation and creativity are necessary."[12]

Some corporations are attempting to reduce the burden of bearing and rearing children. According to *Business Week*, "The Conference Board estimates that 2,500 companies provided some form of childcare aid in 1985, up from 600 in 1982."[13] Only 150 have on-site day-care centers so far, which are expensive and generally full. But some companies are trying alternatives and supplements so that employees can trade information, be referred to an appropriate center, or have their children tended when they're sick.

More major companies are providing maternity leave. Incredibly, according to the October 6, 1986, issue of *Business Week*, only 40 percent of working women can now take a maternity leave, including those who must use their sick and vacation leave. Generally, the policies that companies adopt are more amenable to the family issues women face, although it will be some time before the wrinkles are ironed out. As they are, the pressure on women to balance their family and work responsibilities will ease, at least in some respects.

New programs being instituted in some corporations are also aimed at reducing the pressure of being a woman in a man's world. There are reports of companies that now sponsor workshops to change the attitudes of *male* executives toward affirmative action and women in general. The *Wall Street Journal*'s special supplement on corporate women reported that Merck & Company, Mead Corporation, and others offer programs designed to confront and remedy men's resentment of successful women, from older male executives who think women don't belong in management to begin with to young men who regard women as competitors with an unfair advantage.[14]

One way to change attitudes, some managers believe, is to create a "mass" of women in significant jobs within one part of the company instead of spreading the somewhat few of these women throughout the corporation where each is isolated and scrutinized as the token woman. Nearly 10 percent of our 76 executives said specifically that having female colleagues would have helped them. Taking some of the pressure off in this way could be effective, if it can be done without creating a female ghetto in which none of the female executives is taken seriously. Recall that executives are leery of segregating themselves into a women's camp, so a concentration of women in one part of the business will probably cause concern among themselves as well as others. As companies experiment with various ways of taking some of the heat off executive women, we will all learn more about what does and doesn't work.

Then there are the companies that attack the problem from another angle—substituting internal criteria as a sort of voluntary EEO program to keep women moving up. For instance, Gannett Company now ties managers' bonuses to equal opportunity goals.[15] Edward W. Jones, Jr., an executive turned consultant, wrote a personal account, "What It's Like to Be a Black Manager," and argued, in a follow-up article in the 1986 *Harvard*

Business Review, that measurable criteria are needed for black managers to receive equity, and some agree that that also applies to women:

Corporations cannot manage attitudes, but they can manage behavior with accountability, rewards, and punishment, as in all other important areas of concern. What gets measured in business gets done, what is not measured is ignored.[16]

These are some of the techniques that corporations are turning to in order to keep and use the talent of their female employees. For a change, management is trying to adapt their companies to the needs of women, and the techniques are sometimes very creative. DuPont, for example, runs programs on rape prevention. The genius of such programs is that they convey to women what Lee Iacocca acknowledged to be a crucial part of effective management—they make the employees feel important. The majority of women surveyed in 1982 wanted a job where "people really care about me as a person," yet the majority of management and professional women surveyed in 1985 said they are not made to feel important in the companies they work for.[17]

Programs such as this clearly are no substitute for job assignments that challenge and reward the women who are driven to climb the corporate Everest. Most of our savvy insiders, as well as the 76 women we interviewed, agreed that more line jobs are now going to women and that fast-track women are getting into management positions earlier than they have in the past. And while formal EEO pressure has been reduced, *Fortune* magazine reported in 1985 that more than 95 percent of the 127 Fortune 500 CEOs polled in an Organization Resources Counselors' survey said that they *do* plan to continue to use numerical objectives to track the progress of women and minorities in their companies.[18] And with the earlier start and a growing reluctance in some companies to move women (as well as men) as fast as they have, perhaps women will be better able to take added doses of responsibility at a more consistent and reasonable pace, rather than packing huge changes in job scope into a short span of time.

The combination of desirable job assignments and the package of programs designed to make the workplace less hostile will allow high-potential women to compete on a more equal footing with men for top jobs. Such innovations will reduce the three levels of pressure that sap the strength of executive women. At the very least, they will make the decision many executive women confront—to stay with the company or leave—a bit tougher.

What Women Can Do

Companies are not grappling with the issue alone. The efforts of many, many individuals also are needed to make a significant difference in the prospects for executive women. We believe that if fast-track women relax and assume that they no longer have to meet any special requirements and that the corporate system now wholeheartedly endorses their presence and their ambitions, then it will take even longer for women to reach top management. Simply letting time pass is not the best approach. Continued advocacy for the necessary support systems and their implementation on a much grander scale is one responsibility that falls on the women who are at fairly high levels and who want to lead their corporations as well as on the corporations' other representatives whose mandate it is to find, keep, and use the talent available.

The premier responsibility that women will carry with them for generations to come—the one that will make the most difference in their own careers as well as in the odds that other women will succeed at top jobs—is to be exceptionally and consistently outstanding. "I'm still convinced women have to work harder and longer to get ahead," said one of the 76 executives in our study, one of the group of twice as many who believed that it's just as hard or harder for women today to move up in the company versus those who said things are better for women today.

The generations of women who follow in the footsteps of the corporate trailblazers in our study will do well, we believe, to follow the advice that they offered. It is not surprising that much of their advice is based largely on the pressures they encountered and how they made the developmental leaps that were so important to their own success—the challenges of management, the struggle for acceptance as a minority group member in the executive ranks, and the dilemma of satisfying family and personal needs as well as career needs. The pressures on high-potential women haven't changed so much (nor are they likely to in the foreseeable future) that other women cannot benefit from the experience of the pioneers. We believe they face the same hoops as did their predecessors.

The advice they gave falls into five general categories that may be the five commandments of becoming a top executive:

Commandment 1: Be Able. There is no substitute for competence: to learn the job, basic skills like speaking and writing, and anything else that will help you compete against everyone else at your level. "Take anything that will help you understand how the business works." Continue your education so that your skills don't "grow old." Put in the extra time and effort on every job—"you never know when you're being looked at."

This is the work-hard-and-be-smart criterion that is seen as a necessary but not sufficient condition for reaching the top—it is only about 20 percent of what it takes to move ahead in a corporation. Many women will learn the hard way, as some of our executives did, that much more is required.

Commandment 2: Be *Seen* as Able. Don't let your abilities be discounted or ignored. Display competency in jobs that are visible and valued by getting into line jobs, into the mainstream of the business, into jobs that form stepping-stones to the top. Control your career, take the risks that senior executives admire, and "avoid dead ends." "If you have two ounces of common sense, you can tell if you are in a meaningful part of the corporation. If you're not, get out; go where the action is."

One executive suggested, "Go with a progressive, nonsexist organization and boss. Don't try to change the culture." The message here is to take charge of your own public relations campaign so that your accomplishments are noticed and rewarded. The assignments you take, the training programs you attend, the bosses you work for, the community organizations you preside over, and about everything else tend to have a symbolic meaning in the company. Knowing where to focus your effort is an advantage if not an outright requirement.

Commandment 3: Help Others to Help You. "You can't do it alone" is one of the most frequent revelations among executives; a common piece of advice is to rely on other people—let your subordinates do their jobs, "find a mentor," "never drop networking even if your jobs don't relate," and so on. But knowing who you need is only part of the job. Getting what you need from those people is at least as difficult. "Get a plan, a strategy. Let your boss and others know what it is," so they can contribute to it, not create it for you. The more specific you can be, the easier it is to get some kinds of help. Relying on one person or others in general for too much or too general assistance can be disappointing and even hazardous.

Some executives suggested, "Don't have a chip on your shoulder" that could alienate potential allies. Being gracious, appreciative of help, and generally easy to be with encourages others to help. Encouragement also means not being afraid to ask for advice or the all-important feedback about performance, style, and others' perceptions. Many people are reluctant to criticize (and even to praise!), so it is often necessary to be persistent in obtaining feedback from selected individuals you respect and trust. Once you get the feedback, act on it, assimilate it into your work, and make sure that others know you took their advice.

Commandment 4: Prepare to Be Lucky. "Train yourself beyond the job." "Do a lot of different things. Don't stay in one place too long." Pushing your experience as far and wide as possible, on and off the job, gives you options you wouldn't otherwise have. "Be flexible and open to opportunities" instead of structuring your career too narrowly. One executive advised going on job interviews even if you don't want the job, and another suggested taking lateral moves. Opportunities, after all, are unscheduled and sometimes disguised.

In advising younger managers, our executives didn't talk about luck. It does no good to tell someone to be lucky. Instead, they emphasized controlling what you can control and seeking out windows of opportunity. Clearly, many agree with the male executive from the earlier study who said, "The harder you work, the luckier you get." Perhaps it is understood among executives that sometimes a little luck is the only difference between a successful executive and one who derails.

Commandment 5: Know What You Want. A vice presidency doesn't amount to much for someone who would rather be doing something else. Executives tell others it is necessary to "know what you want out of life" and to balance, prioritize, sacrifice, relax—the advice is about as contradictory as it could be, presumably because the executives individually have adopted different and contrasting techniques for getting personal satisfaction along with career success. Many of them have made difficult choices, fought guilt, and lost opportunities. The best they can do in advising others is usually to recommend what has worked for them (such as delaying children or limiting work to only a few ten-hour days at a time) or suggest that you do some careful soul-searching and act on what you find.

There will be more women making choices that involve general management jobs, and eventually the most senior management positions. The pressure of these choices is staggering: To be one of the few women, if not the only one, at that level? To open more doors for other women? Or to have children and focus on raising a family? To fuel the fires of sexism further by declining advancement? Or to abandon the bureaucracy to be in charge of a small business?

For many women, the difficulty of preparing, excelling, and networking will pale in the face of these life decisions. They must define success more broadly than simply moving up in a corporation. The options that many of our 76 executives are considering will remain tempting for years to come.

Is There Happiness below the Executive Vice President Level?

It is discouraging that so little progress is evident in the accessibility of senior management jobs for women in our largest corporations. More work and more frustration lie ahead before women can reach the top. General management is beginning to open up to more women, and we expect to see the numbers of women at this level increase in this century. But the door will likely remain closed to women at the highest levels of major corporations for at least another generation.

Of course, some women won't be especially hurt by these limits. Success and happiness will come to many women who go back home or start a business or hold a responsible job lower in the company. It isn't easy to evoke a lot of sympathy for a woman who controls millions of dollars of corporate resources and pulls down a $200,000 annual salary. But others will not be content until women, perhaps themselves included, have the same odds that men have. These include people who believe that their corporation's competitive advantage lies in giving women equal opportunities so that they won't lose the best executives they have. With such persistence, there is light at the end of the tunnel for executive women.

Appendix

·
Appendix

Executive Women Project

Seventy-six women in or near general management jobs at twenty-five Fortune 100-sized companies.

- 52 (68 percent) were classified as general managers.
  Typical job titles were
    division president
    senior vice president
    vice president
    general manager

- 24 (32 percent) were classified as one level below general manager.
  Typical job titles were
    director
    district sales manager
    associate/assistant general counsel
    assistant treasurer/comptroller

A companion study was conducted with 22 "savvy insiders"— those responsible for identifying and selecting executives for top jobs—at ten of the same Fortune 100-sized companies.

- 16 (73 percent) were men, and 6 (27 percent) were women. They held line and staff positions in five manufacturing and five service firms.

- They gave us case histories on 19 women who were considered successful and 16 women who were derailed—plateaued, demoted, forced to retire, or fired.

What is a Fortune 100 / Service 100 company?

- We interviewed 45 women (59 percent of the sample) at fifteen Fortune 100 companies. These are manufacturing companies whose sales and assets vary from $4 billion to $56+ billion and $3 billion to $40+ billion, respectively. The median number of employees in these fifteen companies was seventy-nine thousand.

- We interviewed 31 women (41 percent of the sample) at ten Service 100 companies: four banks, five diversified financial, and one retail. The median number of employees was forty-two thousand. The financial profile of these companies compares favorably with the fifteen manufacturing firms.

A Demographic Profile
of 76 Executives

AGE

Age range   30–60
Median age   40

	Range	*N*	*%*
	30–39	37	48.7
	40–49	29	38.2
	50–60	10	13.1

RACE

Black	3	3.9
White	73	96.1

MARITAL STATUS

Married (includes 8 remarried)	56	74.0
Divorced/separated	14	18.0
Single—never married	5	7.0
Unknown	1	1.0

A Demographic Profile
of 76 Executives (*cont.*)

CHILDREN

	N	%
Number with children	37	48.7
1 child	16	
2 children	11	
3 children	5	
4 children	2	
Unknown number	3	
Average number of children	1.8	
Age range of children	5 mos. to 29 years	

CORPORATE TENURE

Average number of years in present company	12.7 years
Average number of years in all companies	15.8 years
Average number of jobs	7.7
Average total management experience	11.7 years

Research Sponsor Program

An earlier study in 1982 by the Center for Creative Leadership, part of the Research Sponsor Program, included interviews with 79 executives at three Fortune 100 companies. All but one of these executives were men. Many of the questions asked of the 79 executives were the same as those asked of the women, and the interviews were conducted in essentially the same way. A description of the earlier study is awaiting publication (McCall, Lombardo, and Morrison).

Comparing successful women and men yields the following profile:

	76 Women		79 Men***	
	N	%	N	%
General manager*	52	(68.4)	55	(69.6)
1 level below general manager	24	(31.6)	24	(30.4)
Line**	28	(36.8)	45	(57.0)
Staff	48	(63.2)	34	(43.0)
General manager/line	24	(31.6)	38	(48.1)
1 level below general manager/line	4	(5.3)	7	(8.9)
General manager/staff	28	(36.8)	17	(21.5)
1 level below general manager/staff	20	(26.3)	17	(21.5)
Age range	30–60		30–65	
Median age	40		47	

*To be considered a general manager, incumbents had to have responsibility for multiple functions (for example, sales *and* marketing) or for heading a business unit. If they had responsibility for a single function, they had to be at corporate headquarters with all divisions reporting to them.

**Line and staff classification was industry-specific and sometimes company-specific. Areas evaluated as support—personnel, human resources, finance, legal, and occasionally marketing—were considered staff. Manufacturing, operations, sales, marketing, and finance (in service industries) were areas that made a direct contribution to profits or losses. Incumbents holding these positions were considered line executives. For the women, 39 (51 percent) had had line experience at some time during their careers.

***The positions of the 79 executives interviewed in the 1982 study were reanalyzed according to the criteria used in the Executive Women Project.

Executive Women Project
Interview Questions

From November 1984 to May 1985, we interviewed 22 "savvy insiders"—those responsible for identifying and selecting executives for top jobs—from ten of the same Fortune 100 companies: five manufacturing and five service. Of the 22 top executives, 16 were men, and 6 were women. On average, the interviews lasted two hours. Each interview was transcribed by the interviewer (we did not tape-record the interview).

PREPARATION

Please think of two women whose careers you know pretty well: one who made it to the top of your company—that is, into the general management ranks (perhaps even the highest ten or so positions)—and one who was seen as top management material and either (a) didn't make it or (b) made it and was not successful. The second person should be someone who did in fact attain a fairly high management position.

Both executives you select should be

- women you know pretty well, so that you have a good perspective on their careers, and
- women who are reasonably representative, in the sense that you believe the forces propelling them to the top (or putting on the brakes) are fairly typical in your organization. We know that each case is in some ways unique; what we hope to avoid are the really unusual cases.

The two women you select may be past or current incumbents, but they should be contemporaries, hopefully within the past five or so years.

SECTION I: CONTRASTS

First let's consider the woman who "made it" to the top.

1. Briefly tell us what you know about this woman's career (a sketch).

2. How did this woman first catch the eye of important managers in the company? What kinds of things did she do that held their attention over the years?

3. What do you see as the critical turning points in this woman's career (how did she "earn her wings"):
   • as a young (or new) manager
   • in the middle levels
   • in the executive suite

4. How has she changed significantly over the course of her career:
   • for the better
   • for the worse

5. How and when did assessment of this person's potential change over time?

6. Did this person ever make a big mistake and then recover from it? How did she recover?

7. Once this woman was recognized as a viable candidate for a high-level job, did she get any special attention? Was she, for example, given special assignments, challenges, or bosses because of her potential?

8. When did she first realize that she was considered to be a candidate for a top job? Did this knowledge have an effect on her? Did the company ever recognize her in a formal way? Did that have any effect?

9. What other people played a significant part in her career success? How?

10. What single thing do you think contributed most to this woman's ultimate success in getting to the top?

11. How representative is this woman of those who make it to the top in your company? How does she differ from the men who make it?

Now let's look at the woman who "derailed" (was seen as a high-potential candidate for a top job but failed either to achieve that level or to succeed at that level).

1. Briefly tell us what you know about this woman's career (a sketch).
2. Obviously this person achieved a great deal in the company, even if she never attained what was hoped by management. What were key events that contributed to that success—what led to this person being seen as high-potential and attaining the level she did?
3. What was the sequence of events that led to derailing from the track to the top jobs?
4. What happened to this woman afterward?
5. How representative is this person of women who get derailed? How does she differ from the men who derail?

SECTION 2: OTHER EXPERIENCES

We have dealt with two specific examples, but your experience with high-potential female executives is probably broader than that.

1. Can you think of other examples that would help us better understand the road to the top:
   a. Examples of critical career turning points—events that had a significant impact on a woman's growth or advancement.
   b. Examples of "fatal flaws"—things that caused high-potential women to derail along the road to the top.

SECTION 3: GENERAL QUESTIONS

1. Do you believe some parts of the company are more likely to produce top female executives than others? Which ones, and why?

2. Are there certain specific jobs or types of jobs you see as critically important in "seasoning" female managers on the way up?

3. Are there certain jobs or types of assignments that can enhance a woman's credibility in the company, as opposed to her skill or knowledge per se? How do they help?

4. Do you think the "road to the top" is different for women today from what it was for women in the past? Do you think it will change in the future?

5. Do you believe the best women make it? That is, among the pool of female candidates, do you think the most competent are selected for executive positions?

6. Are there other factors or events we haven't already covered that you think are important in understanding why some women continue upward into top jobs and others don't?

Success Factors Most Frequently Mentioned
by Savvy Insiders

	Percentage of the 19 Success Cases	*Percentage of the 16 Derailment Cases*
Help from above	100%	38%
Track record	89%	88%
Drive to succeed	84%	44%
Ability to manage subordinates	74%	—
Willingness to take career risks	74%	—
Tough, decisive, demanding	68%	13%
Smart	58%	63%
Impressive image	58%	19%
Works through others	58%	6%
Adapts to environment	53%	25%
Easy to be with	53%	13%

Appendix

Flaws Most Frequently Mentioned by Savvy Insiders

	Percentage of the 16 Derailment Cases	*Percentage of the 19 Success Cases*
Unable to adapt*	50%	21%
Performance problem*	50%	21%
Wants too much/too ambitious*	50%	11%
Can't manage subordinates	44%	26%
Poor relationships	38%	32%
Not strategic	38%	5%
Poor image	38%	5%

*Fifteen of the 16 derailment cases (94%) had at least one of these three flaws.

Derailment Factors:
A Comparison of Derailed Women and Men*
Described by Savvy Insiders

	Derailed Women Said to Have This Flaw (total is 16)	Derailed Men Said to Have This Flaw (total is 20)
Unable to adapt	8 (50%)	7 (35%)
Performance problem	8 (50%)	13 (65%)
Wants too much/too ambitious	8 (50%)	4 (20%)
Unable to lead subordinates	7 (44%)	7 (35%)
Not strategic	6 (38%)	5 (25%)
Presented a poor image	6 (38%)	1 (5%)
Poor relationships	6 (38%)	20 (100%)
Skill deficits	5 (31%)	4 (20%)
Not driven to succeed	4 (25%)	2 (10%)
Too narrow	3 (19%)	—

*The data for the men were collected at three Fortune 100 corporations as part of an earlier study conducted at the Center for Creative Leadership. Nineteen savvy insiders were interviewed and gave detailed descriptions of twenty success cases and twenty cases of derailment. Data for derailed men were reanalyzed using categories developed in the Executive Women Project. One incomplete case from the original men's data was dropped.

A Comparison of Successful Women and Men*
Described by Savvy Insiders

	Number and Percentage of 19 Successful Women	*Number and Percentage of 20 Successful Men*
Help from above	19 (100%)	11 (55%)
Desire to succeed	16 (84%)	9 (45%)
Took career risks	14 (74%)	3 (15%)
Tough, decisive, demanding	13 (68%)	4 (20%)
Impressive image	11 (58%)	5 (25%)
Easy to be with	10 (53%)	4 (20%)
Able to adapt to the environment	10 (53%)	—
Track record	17 (89%)	15 (75%)
Can manage subordinates	14 (74%)	10 (50%)
Smart	11 (58%)	14 (70%)
Works through others	11 (58%)	12 (60%)

*The data for the men were collected at three Fortune 100 corporations as part of an earlier study conducted at the Center for Creative Leadership. Nineteen savvy insiders were interviewed and gave detailed descriptions of twenty success cases and twenty cases of derailment. Data for derailed men were reanalyzed using categories developed in the Executive Women Project. One incomplete case from the original men's data was dropped.

Psychological and Behavioral
Assessment Profiles
of Executive Men and Women

The following two tables present psychological and behavioral assessment data on another sample of executive women and men. These data were drawn from the 1978–86 Center for Creative Leadership data base. The sample comprises women and men at or above the upper middle management level in businesses with at least five thousand employees. The California Personality Inventory, designed to measure dispositions relevant to social interaction, was administered to participants prior to the Leadership Development Program. The Shipley Institute of Living Scale and the two behavioral assessment exercises were undertaken on the first day of the program. The Shipley is a measure of cognitive ability, while the behavioral assessment exercises provide information on how people behave in group problem-solving meetings when there is a high level of ambiguity in terms of role and purpose. Both behavioral assessments are leaderless group discussions, with six people given a problem to solve and then left alone to work out a solution. The first problem is competitive in nature, with resources such that only one person's solution can prevail. The second problem is cooperative, in that the group members must pool their resources to achieve a solution. During these exercises, each participant is observed by a trained rater and is assigned a score on each of the eight dimensions listed on the behavioral assessment table.

California Personality Inventory
(Leadership Development Program Participants)

Subscale	Executive Women (N=31) Mean (Standard Deviation)	Executive Men (N=393) Mean (Standard Deviation)	Comparison*
Dominance	61 (10.8)	64 (8.8)	=
Capacity for status	57 (10.4)	55 (8.0)	=
Sociability	52 (11.7)	53 (9.0)	=
Social presence	55 (10.8)	56 (9.9)	=
Self-acceptance	58 (9.0)	61 (8.3)	=
Sense of well-being	46 (11.9)	53 (8.2)	w < m
Responsibility	48 (9.7)	50 (8.9)	=
Socialization	45 (11.8)	50 (8.2)	w < m
Self-control	47 (7.7)	50 (8.9)	=
Tolerance	51 (8.5)	53 (7.5)	=
Good impression	47 (8.6)	49 (9.8)	=
Communality	46 (11.8)	54 (7.5)	w < m
Achievement via conformance	52 (9.8)	56 (7.6)	w < m
Achievement via independence	57 (8.7)	59 (8.1)	=
Intellectual efficiency	50 (13.2)	53 (8.4)	=
Psychological mindedness	58 (8.5)	58 (8.7)	=
Flexibility	56 (12.1)	53 (10.3)	=

*">" or "<" indicates statistical significance at the alpha <.05 level.

Shipley Institute of Living Scale
(Leadership Development Program Participants)

	Executive Women (N = 25)	Executive Men (N = 327)	Comparison*
Total score	119 (7.1)	120 (7.3)	—

*">" or "<" indicates statistical significance at the alpha <.05 level.

Behavioral Assessment Data
(Leadership Development Program Participants)

	Executive Women (N = 26)	Executive Men (N = 331)	
Assessment I *Competitive* *Group Exercise*	*Mean (Standard Deviation)*	*Mean (Standard Deviation)*	*Comparison**
Activity level	35 (9.3)	35 (6.7)	=
Led the discussion	34 (9.4)	33 (6.9)	=
Influenced others	34 (9.1)	34 (6.6)	=
Problem analysis	35 (8.9)	35 (6.0)	=
Task orientation	34 (8.3)	35 (6.3)	=
Motivated others	34 (9.5)	32 (6.6)	=
Interpersonal skills	34 (8.6)	33 (5.2)	=
Verbal effectiveness	38 (8.9)	36 (4.8)	=
Assessment II *Cooperative* *Group Exercise*			
Activity level	39 (5.5)	36 (6.1)	w > m
Led the discussion	37 (6.8)	34 (6.7)	=
Influenced others	37 (6.0)	35 (6.4)	=
Problem analysis	36 (5.9)	35 (6.1)	=
Task orientation	38 (5.5)	36 (5.7)	=
Motivated others	36 (6.0)	34 (6.7)	=
Interpersonal skills	34 (4.4)	34 (4.8)	=
Verbal effectiveness	38 (3.8)	37 (4.9)	=

*">" or "<" indicates statistical significance at the alpha <.05 level.

Management Skills Profile*

The Management Skills Profile (MSP) is an instrument that focuses on specific, job-related skills required for management success. It requires that an individual manager, his or her immediate supervisor, one to three subordinates, and one to three peers rate the manager's skills on 122 items, comprising 19 scale scores.

The data presented here were provided by Personnel Decisions, Inc., in Minneapolis, Minnesota. The sample is comprised of 175 male and 19 female managers at the executive level in manufacturing, service, or retail firms. The data were collected during the period 1982 to 1986, inclusive.

*Personnel Decisions, Inc., Minneapolis, Minnesota, holds the copyright (1982) on the Management Skills Profile.

Management Skills Profile:
Management Skills Definitions

COGNITIVE

Problem Analysis and Decision Making Identifying problems; recognizing symptoms, causes, and alternative solutions; making timely, sound decisions even under conditions of risk and uncertainty.

Financial and Quantitative Analysis Drawing accurate conclusions from financial and numerical material and applying financial principles and numerical techniques to management problems.

ADMINISTRATIVE

Planning Setting goals and developing strategies and schedules for meeting those goals; anticipating obstacles and defining alternative strategies.

Organizing Scheduling and coordinating work of others; setting priorities; establishing efficient work procedures to meet objectives.

Personal Organization, Time Management, and Handling Detail Allocating one's own time efficiently; arranging information systematically and processing paperwork and other information effectively without getting bogged down in detail.

COMMUNICATIONS

Informing Letting people know of decisions, changes, and other relevant information on a timely basis.

Oral Communications Speaking effectively one to one and in groups; making effective presentations.
Listening Demonstrating attention to, and conveying understanding of, the comments or questions of others.
Written Communications Writing clearly and effectively; using appropriate style, grammar, and tone in informal and formal business communications.

INTERPERSONAL

Human Relations Developing and maintaining smooth, cooperative working relationships with peers, subordinates, and superiors; showing awareness of, and consideration for, the opinions and feeling of others.
Managing Conflict and Confrontation Bringing conflict or dissent into the open and using it productively to enhance the quality of decisions; arriving at constructive solutions while maintaining positive working relationships.

LEADERSHIP

Leadership Style and Influence Taking charge and initiating actions, directing the activities of individuals and groups toward the accomplishment of meaningful goals, and commanding the attention and respect of others.
Motivating Others Creating an environment in which subordinates and others are rewarded for accomplishment of group and individual goals.
Delegating and Controlling Clearly assigning responsibilities and tasks to others and establishing effective controls, ensuring that employees have the necessary resources and authority, and monitoring progress and exercising control.
Coaching and Developing Evaluating employees, providing performance feedback, and facilitating professional growth.

PERSONAL MOTIVATION

Displaying a high energy level, working long and hard to get things done, and seeking increased responsibility on the job.

PERSONAL ADAPTABILITY

Responding appropriately and competently to the demands of work challenges when confronted with changes, ambiguity, adversity, or other pressures.

OCCUPATIONAL/TECHNICAL KNOWLEDGE

Applying the knowledge and skills needed to do the job, including technical competence in one's own field and familiarity with policies and practices of the organization and the industry.

© Personnel Decisions, Inc., 1982

Management Skills Profile
Sex Differences by Rater Perspective

Rater Perspective

Scale	Supervisor	Subordinate	Peer	Self
Planning	=	=	=	=
Organizing	=	=	=	=
Personal organization/time management	=	=	=	=
Informing	=	=	=	m < w*
Oral communications	=	=	=	=
Listening	=	=	=	=
Written communications	=	=	=	m < w
Problem analysis/ decision making	=	=	=	=
Financial/ quantitative	=	=	=	m > w
Human relations	=	=	=	=
Managing conflict/ confrontation	=	=	=	=
Leadership style/ influence	=	=	=	=
Motivating others	=	=	=	=
Delegating and controlling	=	=	=	=
Coaching and developing	=	=	=	=
Personal motivation	=	=	=	=

*">" or "<" indicates statistical significance at the alpha < .01 level.

Management Skills Profile
Sex Differences by Rater Perspective (*cont.*)

	Rater Perspective			
Scale	*Supervisor*	*Subordinate*	*Peer*	*Self*
Personal adaptability	=	=	=	=
Occupational/ technical knowledge	=	=	=	=
Results orientation	=	=	=	m < w

Interview Questions

From November 1984 to May 1985, we conducted interviews with 76 successful executives. Each interviewee received the twenty-three questions one week prior to the scheduled interview. On average, the interviews lasted two hours. Each interview was transcribed by the interviewer (we did not tape-record the interview).

SECTION I

When you think about your career as a manager, certain events or episodes probably stand out in your mind—things that led to a lasting change in you as a manager. Please jot down some notes for yourself identifying at least three "key events" in your career; things that made a difference in the way you manage now. When we meet with you, we'll ask you about each event:

1. What happened?
   What did you learn from it (for better or worse)?

Please identify three events before proceeding to the next section.

SECTION II: KEY EVENTS

Having thought about key events that really stood out for you, we'll now address some things that may or may not have had a lasting effect on you. What happened? What did you learn from the experience?

As you look over the questions, some are no doubt more meaningful to you than others. Please be prepared to go into some depth on the important ones, and comment only briefly on the others. Still other questions may have been answered in the first section.

A. Rites of Passage

1. What was your first managerial job? Was there anything special about it? What did you learn from it?

2. What was your first "quantum leap"—movement to a job with significantly more responsibility/challenge/pressure than prior jobs?

3. What was your first important exposure to high-level executives? What did you learn?

4. What is the biggest challenge you have ever faced?

5. What was your most frightening first—something you did for the first time that really had you worried?

B. Rising from the Ashes

1. What was your darkest hour?

2. Tell me about a time when you tried something that was important to you and failed.

3. What was your most significant act of procrastination? By this we mean a time when you didn't face up to a situation that got steadily worse, resulting in a mess.

4. Were you ever worn out or fed up, but managed to restart? How?

C. The Role of Other People

1. Please describe the person who taught you the most during your career. What did that person do that made him or her so special?

2. Most of us have worked for a person we simply couldn't tolerate for one reason or another. What did you learn from such an experience?

3. What was your most significant interpersonal conflict—
a situation in which dealing with another person (or persons) was very difficult for you? What did you learn from it?

SECTION III: GENERAL QUESTIONS

1. Sometimes people have experiences outside of work that impact them as managers. What part have events in your personal life played in your growth as a manager?
2. What kinds of personal sacrifices have you had to make to get where you are today?
3. What advice would you give to a younger manager about managing her own career?
4. What one important thing about your career do you think would have been different were you a man? An example?
5. Have your business or career decisions been affected by the fact that what you do could impact women who follow in your footsteps? How?
6. Do you see yourself as a role model for other women? In what way(s)?
7. Is there something your company did to help you succeed? Is there something your company could have done?
8. Sometimes people invest in developmental activities that they hope will pay off for them. Can you think of something you did specifically to help you develop that proved to be particularly valuable? How about something that turned out to be a waste of time?
9. Where do you see your career moving? What's next for you?
10. Is there something we should have asked you but didn't?

Key Events
Reported by 76 Executive Women

SIGNIFICANT JOB CHANGES

First Management Job (17 of 261 Key Events): These range from first supervisory slots to vice president. Most include mention of a special boss (either helpful or a hindrance) and sometimes involve a huge leap in responsibility—either by title or doing something that the company has never done before. Supervising older, more experienced, and/or male employees and establishing credibility are among the issues faced by first-time managers.

First "Real" Management or General Manager Job (17 Key Events): Moving into a job where the manager has to manage significantly more people, functions, or budget (sometimes for the first time). Subordinates may be geographically dispersed. Managers report being the first/only woman at this level and face a variety of problems, such as managing in an area in which they lack technical competence; peers, boss, or subordinates have to be won over; reorganization/housecleaning is necessary.

Rocky Road (20 Key Events): Problems encountered when trying to make a career/job change—being passed over, a boss blocking a job change, staff making the environment uncomfortable, prejudice that a woman couldn't do a job, fighting for recognition or a new job, and fighting for pay. Most of the events have positive outcomes. The two that didn't are positive in that the individuals received the job they wanted, but their experiences in the new job were unpleasant.

Career Change (18 Key Events):   These involve pursuing new interests—moving to a different function within an operation, moving to a different division within the company, changing companies, or leaving academia or government for the corporate world. These changes are often seen as "risky" but provide exciting challenge, often launching the executive in a new direction.

Move to Corporate Staff (10 Key Events):   Taking on and learning how to perform in a corporate staff position. Most involve daily contact with top executives and a tremendous increase in work load due both to the job being much broader and to the fact that many are managing high-level people for the first time. These jobs gave the manager great visibility and exposure throughout the organization.

Staff to Line (5 Key Events):   Moving from a staff to a line position. These usually involve moving from having responsibility for analysis, service, or support to having clear responsibility for profit and loss, implementation, and bottom-line decision making. Some involve a technical area with which the manager is unfamiliar.

Other Promotions (5 Key Events):   These are high-level promotions that do not fall into other categories—a move into a new area, a step up the ladder, or a change in company. Three women were promoted to vice president; 2 were promoted to the director level.

OTHER PEOPLE

Helpful Bosses (26 Key Events):   Being positively influenced or helped by direct boss(es), who often served as role models that the executives emulated and provided opportunities for the executives to try new things, to get recognized, and to get promoted. Some even took on an active role as adviser and coach.

Helpful Others (11 Key Events): The helpful others are mostly family members (with husbands and fathers most frequently mentioned) and others from the organization in positions above the executive. Helpful others are not peers or friends and are typically older or more experienced than the executive. The help was provided over an extended period of time, taking more than one form and having a big influence on the executive's image of herself as a manager.

Bad Bosses (18 Key Events): Bosses who were said to be insecure, to overmanage, to lack people skills, or to be untrustworthy or inept either interpersonally or technically. In several cases, the "bad" boss replaced a boss who was remembered in favorable terms as helpful and supportive.

HASSLES AND DISAPPOINTMENTS

Confronting Problem Employees (10 Key Events): These are cases in which the executives experienced difficulty with one or a group of subordinates. Not always direct confrontations with the individual(s), the problems involve substance abuse, adjustment to the executive being in charge, poor performance, and inability to accept the executive's management style.

Firing a Problem Employee (7 Key Events): Terminating an employee. In five cases, there was perceived pressure not to fire the subordinate because he or she was black, a woman, or described as brilliant. In four cases, it was a successful power play on the part of the woman to show her power.

Making a Mistake (9 Key Events): Mistakes made on the job that hurt the executives' business performance and/or relationships with coworkers. Most of the failures happened while the executives were trying to prove themselves—they took on projects that were too big or too sophisticated for them. Some lost touch with key subordinates who didn't follow through or left the company, and one lost touch with her boss—she failed to tell him about a problem. Some weren't effective team players—their independence, hostility, and concern for being right cost them a boss's trust, a state-of-the-art project, and even a merit bonus. Interpersonal problems and not involving the right people are key themes in most of these events.

A Conflict (8 Key Events): Interpersonal conflicts with peers, bosses, and senior-level executives. Five were confrontations with peers; two of these were later viewed by the executive as a mistake. The conflicts with a boss and senior executive were instances where the executive was being sabotaged. Most conflicts were seen by the executive as caused by the other person.

Missing a Promotion (6 Key Events): Being passed over for promotion or (in one case) denied tenure despite excellent credentials. These executives feel they were denied something they deserved because of their credentials, talents, or experience. Four cited sex discrimination as a factor in losing out.

CHALLENGING ASSIGNMENTS

Fix-It (6 Key Events): These involve taking over a department or business that had serious problems and turning it around. They cut costs, changed personnel, improved the image, dealt with increased competition. In two cases, it was also their first time managing people.

Negotiation (7 Key Events): Successes in a negotiation situation. They involved winning acceptance in a negotiating role overseas; convincing others to accept a program, opinion, or project; or opening the doors for continued negotiation as in a union grievance procedure.

Chair Task Force or Team (6 Key Events):   Taking charge of a very visible group to solve a major problem confronting the organization. Three dealt with issues of high visibility outside the organization. These managers had to win cooperation and consensus at several levels in the organization, and to manage laterally and upward.

Other Assignments (7 Key Events):   These are presentations, closing down part of a business or an entire business, starting a new operation, or traveling overseas.

GETTING TUNED IN

Getting Feedback (13 Key Events):   Receiving feedback (both positive and negative) from bosses, peers, and subordinates about managerial style and performance. Most of the feedback given was used by the executives in a constructive way.

Milestones in Corporate Savvy (10 Key Events):   Getting acquainted with the system—learning the ropes about corporate politics, often revealing "ahas" about corporate decision making, corporate values, and corporate culture. These executives learned the value of having early exposure to senior executives, living within the value system, receiving help in promotions, "tooting your own whistle," and the importance of being accepted.

OFF-THE-JOB

Having Children (6 Key Events):   Having a child, usually the executive's first child. The challenge of managing the child along with everything else, or the pregnancy itself, affected these executives' attitudes, behaviors, and career decisions. Setting priorities for yourself—doing what *you* want—is a major theme. These are stressful, even traumatic times.

Family Changes and Relocation (7 Key Events): Decisions about family status or significant relationships, such as breaking up with a husband or moving away from a lover. Most are negative, even devastating events, such as divorces.

Coursework (10 Key Events): Educational programs undertaken by the executives, most of which are outside the company and geared toward a business/management curriculum. The majority are prestigious programs for which the executives were selected, usually with the company's support and funding. Their duration ranged from less than a week for a high-potential manager's assessment program to a two-year MBA program, with more than half being at least a year. Being a woman in these male-dominated programs was often an important factor.

Note: Two events were classified as "miscellaneous" because they did not fit any of the twenty-four categories defined above.

15 Lessons Most Frequently Reported
by 76 Executive Women
and the Key Events that Teach Them

	Major Source(s) of the Lesson	Other Frequent Source(s) of the Lesson
How to deal with people to get things done	Helpful bosses	Helpful others
How to manage: understand/support your people	Confronting a problem employee	Bad bosses
How to manage: general	Helpful bosses	First management job
Take control of your own career	Rocky road	Milestones in corporate savvy
Tenacity and patience	Bad bosses	Career change Rocky road
Self-confidence: general	First management job Helpful bosses	Career change
Take a stand	Rocky road Bad bosses	
Realizing the complexity of the management role	First real management or general manager job	First management job

	Major Source(s) of the Lesson	*Other Frequent Source(s) of the Lesson*
Personal awareness of job-related likes, motives, and goals	First management job	
How to manage: motivate people	First management job	Career change First real management or general manager job Confronting a problem employee
How to manage: develop team/people	First real management or general manager job Helpful bosses	Bad bosses
Understanding senior executives/top management jobs	Move to corporate staff	Helpful bosses
It takes more than smarts and hard work	Milestones in corporate savvy	Rocky road
Importance and technique of networking	Rocky road	First management job Career change Bad bosses
What my weaknesses/ limits are	Rocky road	Mistake/failure

"Extras" of the General Managers*

	Number and Percentage of 52 General Managers
A. Credibility and Presence	
1. Relate as peers outside the company	15 (29%)
2. In a special part of the business	10 (19%)
3. Had prestige degree/education	21 (40%)
4. Exposed to senior executives as an "expert"	28 (54%)
B. Advocacy and Support	
5. EEO/AA helped in her career	20 (38%)
6. Had help, support, advice from boss(es)	18 (35%)
7. Had senior management help	14 (27%)
C. A Break or Two	
8. The business was reorganized, merged, or deregulated	13 (25%)

*These "extras" were counted if it was clear from the interviews that these managers had them. The range in number of "extras" is 0 to 5. Two of the 52 general managers reported no "extras" in their interviews. The average number for each manager was 2.7.

Interview Questions Summary

The following are summaries of the 76 executives' responses to six of the interview questions referred to in the text.

What advice would you give to a younger manager about managing her own career?

	Number and Percentage of Executives Who Gave This Advice[1]
1. Be Able (e.g., learn the business; basic skills; put in extra time, effort)	37 (49%)
2. Be *Seen* as Able (e.g., display competency in visible jobs; control career; go where action is; get into line jobs)	40 (53%)
3. Help Others Help You (e.g., rely on others, delegate; find mentor, network; get plan and let boss know)	38 (50%)
4. Prepare to Be Lucky (e.g., be flexible, open to opportunities; interview and move frequently)	23 (30%)
5. Know What You Want (e.g., know self; prioritize; be a woman, not a man; soul-search; relax)	45 (59%)

What kinds of personal sacrifices have you had to make to get where you are today?

	Number and Percentage of Executives Who Mentioned This[2]
1. Personal time/free time	27 (38%)
2. Social time/friendships	25 (35%)
3. Time with family/children	17[3] (24%)
4. Time with husband/strained marital relationship	14 (20%)
5. Not having children or delaying childbearing	8 (11%)
6. None	16 (23%)

Have your business or career decisions been affected by the fact that what you do may impact women who follow in your footsteps?

	Number and Percentage of Executives Who Mentioned This[4]
Yes	28 (39%)
Conscious of way I conduct myself, know I'm under scrutiny	
Tried to stay in line [job]; break ground	
Staying in current job—want to leave, but would look bad	
Not Really, But . . .	15 (21%)
Know I am visible/failure will impact other women's chances	
No	29 (40%)
Make decisions based on what's best for me	
Don't want responsibility of being trailblazer	
Don't show favoritism toward women	

Do you see yourself as a role model for other women?

	Number and Percentage of Executives Who Mentioned This[5]
1. Yes, and actively try to be	27 (39%)
2. Yes, by virtue of my position	15 (22%)
3. No, but other people say I am	14 (20%)
4. Unsure	11 (16%)
5. No, and I don't want to be	2 (3%)

. . . Are you a mentor to someone?

1. Yes	28 (41%)
2. No	27 (39%)
3. Unsure	9 (13%)
4. No response	5 (7%)

What has your company done to help you succeed?

	Number and Percentage of Executives Who Mentioned This[6]
1. A change/career opportunity (e.g., being hired, promoted, given assignment)	46 (66%)
2. Training/education External/prestige programs Internal/other	28 (40%)
3. Support (e.g., being pushed/encouraged by advocate)	16 (23%)

What more could your company have done?

	Number and Percentage of Executives Who Mentioned This
1. Support/sensitivity/compassion	28 (40%)
2. More/different career opportunities	17 (24%)
3. Guidance/coaching (re: learning the ropes, choosing jobs, give information/feedback)	17 (24%)
4. Nothing more—did everything possible	15 (21%)
5. Training/education (e.g., management/external)	11 (16%)

Where do you see your career moving? What's next for you?

	Number and Percentage of General Managers[7]
1. Few limits—can go higher	15 (30%)
2. Perhaps can go one level higher	11 (22%)
3. Topped out/cannot go higher—not by choice	11 (22%)
4. Plan to opt out/leave the company—by choice	6 (12%)
5. Don't know	7 (14%)

[1]Percentages total more than 100 because most of the 76 respondents offered more than one piece of advice.

[2]In five of the seventy-six interviews, this question was not asked due to a lack of time. The category percentages listed here reflect the percentage of the 71 who did respond. The total exceeds 100 percent because individuals gave multiple responses.

[3]This comprises about half of the 37 women who have children.

[4]In four of the seventy-six interviews, this question was not asked due to a lack of time. The category percentages listed here reflect the percentage of the 72 who did respond.

[5]In seven of the seventy-six interviews, this question was not asked due to a lack of time. The category percentages reflect the percentage of the 69 who did respond.

[6]In six of the seventy-six interviews, this question was not asked due to a lack of time. The category percentages listed here reflect the percentage of the 70 who did respond. The column totals are greater than 100 percent because individuals gave multiple responses.

[7]The data presented here comprise the responses of only the 52 executives who have already reached the general manager level. Fifty of the 52 responded to this question.

Notes

Chapter 1

1. Donald D. Bowen and Robert D. Hisrich, "The Female Entrepreneur: A Career Development Perspective," *Academy of Management Review* 11 (1986): 393.

2. Marilyn Elias, "Corporate Climb Steep for Women," *USA Today*, 22 September 1986, p. 1.

3. Karen Blumenthal, "Room at the Top," *Wall Street Journal*, 24 March 1986, p. 7D.

4. Maggie McComas, "Atop the *Fortune* 500: A Survey of the C.E.O.s," *Fortune*, 28 April 1986, p. 31.

5. John Dubois, "1 in 3 Management Women Drops Out," *USA Today*, 31 July 1986, p. 1.

6. Wendy Leopold, "Top Management Jobs Still an All-Male Organization," *Greensboro* (N.C.) *News and Record*, 7 September 1986, p. E2.

7. Hilary Cosell, *Woman on a Seesaw: The Ups and Downs of Making It* (New York: Putnam, 1985), p. 135.

8. "Even Bosses Unwind; At Least Some Do, Some of the Time," *Wall Street Journal*, 5 August 1986, p. 1.

9. Rosabeth Moss Kanter, *Men and Women of the Corporation* (New York: Basic Books, 1977), p. 239.

10. Ann Morrison, Randall P. White, and Ellen Van Velsor, "The Glass House Dilemma: Why Women Executives Dare Not Fail," *Working Woman* (October 1986): 146.

11. "After the Sexual Revolution," *ABC News Closeup*, 30 July 1986.

12. Charles Margerison and Andrew Kakabadse, *How American Chief Executives Succeed: Implications for Developing High-Potential Employees*, An AMA Survey Report (New York: American Management Associations, 1984), p. 25.

13. Anne Harlan and Carol Weiss, *Moving Up: Women in Managerial Careers*, Working Paper no. 86 (Wellesley, Mass.: Wellesley College, Center for Research on Women, September 1981), p. 99.

14. Norman N. Mlachak, "Life with the CEO," *Industry Week*, 1 October 1984, p. 75.

15. Cosell, *Woman on a Seesaw*, p. 188.

16. Jane Evans, "Leadership—A New Role for Women" (Speech given to the New York Financial Women's Association, 3 June 1986).

Chapter 2

1. *New Yorker* (Issue unknown).

2. Rosabeth Moss Kanter, *Men and Women of the Corporation* (New York: Basic Books, 1977), p. 182.

3. Steven Findlay, "'Male' Career Women," *USA Today*, 13 September 1984, p. 1.

4. Basia Hellwig, "The Breakthrough Generation: 73 Women Ready to Run Corporate America," *Working Woman* (April 1985): 99.

5. *Korn/Ferry International's Profile of Women Senior Executives* (New York: Korn/Ferry International, 1982), p. 20.

6. Julia Kagan, "Who Succeeds, Who Doesn't," *Working Woman* (October 1985): 156.

7. Sey Chassler, "The Women Who Succeed," *Working Woman* (January 1986): 87.

8. Kanter, *Men and Women of the Corporation,* p. 229.

9. Edward W. Jones, Jr., "Black Managers: The Dream Deferred," *Harvard Business Review* 64 (May–June 1986): 84–93.

10. Georgia P. Childress, "Myths and Realities of Women in Management," *Organization Development Journal* 4 (Spring 1986): 44–48.

11. Susan Fraker, "Why Women Aren't Getting to the Top," *Fortune,* 16 April 1984, pp. 40–45. Geraldine Spruell, "Making It, Big Time—Is It Really Tougher for Women?" *Training and Development Journal* 39 (July 1985): 30–33.

12. Morgan W. McCall, Jr., and Michael M. Lombardo, "What Makes a Top Executive?" *Psychology Today* 17 (February 1983): 26–31.

Chapter 3

1. Marilyn Loden, *Feminine Leadership, or, How to Succeed in Business without Being One of the Boys* (New York: Times Books, 1985).

2. Catalyst, *Female Management Style: Myth and Reality* (New York: Catalyst, April 1986).

3. Anne Harlan and Carol Weiss, *Moving Up: Women in Managerial Careers*, Working Paper no. 86 (Wellesley, Mass.: Wellesley College, Center for Research on Women, September 1981), p. 19.

4. Louise Bernikow, "We're Dancing as Fast as We Can," *Savvy* 5 (April 1984): 42.

5. Charlotte Decker Sutton and Kris K. Moore, "Executive Women—20 Years Later," *Harvard Business Review* 63 (September–October 1985): 42–66. Alex Taylor III, "Why Women Managers Are Bailing Out," *Fortune*, 18 August 1986, pp. 16–23.

6. Harlan and Weiss, *Moving Up*, pp. 51, 63.

7. Carol Hymowitz, "Many Blacks Jump Off the Corporate Ladder to Be Entrepreneurs," *Wall Street Journal*, 2 August 1984, p. 1. Larry Reibstein, "Many Hurdles, Old and New, Keep Black Managers out of Top Jobs," *Wall Street Journal*, 10 July 1986, p. 25.

8. Ibid.

Chapter 6

1. Basia Hellwig, "The Breakthrough Generation: 73 Women Ready to Run Corporate America," *Working Woman* (April 1985): 148.

2. Rosabeth Moss Kanter, *Men and Women of the Corporation* (New York: Basic Books, 1977), p. 184.

3. Howard Garland and Kenneth H. Price, "Attitudes toward Women in Management and Attributions for Their Success and Failure in a Managerial Position," *Journal of Applied Psychology* 62 (1977): 30.

4. Pamela Sherrid, "Embarrassment of Riches," *Forbes*, 9 April 1984, pp. 45–46.

Chapter 7

1. Susan Fraker, "Why Women Aren't Getting to the Top," *Fortune*, 16 April 1984, p. 45.

2. Alex Taylor III, "Why Women Managers Are Bailing Out," *Fortune*, 18 August 1986, p. 16.

3. Steven P. Galante, "Venturing Out on Their Own," *Wall Street Journal*, 24 March 1986, p. 4D.

4. Julia Kagan, "Cracks in the Glass Ceiling: How Women Really Are Faring in Corporate America," *Working Woman* (October 1986): 107.

5. Fraker, "Why Women Aren't Getting to the Top," p. 45.

Chapter 8

1. Jane Evans, "Leadership—A New Role for Women" (Speech given to the New York Financial Women's Association, 3 June 1986).

2. Susan Fraker, "Why Women Aren't Getting to the Top," *Fortune*, 16 April 1984, p. 40.

3. Rochelle Distelheim, "The New Shoot-out at Generation Gap," *Working Woman* (March 1986): 113–117, 142–143.

4. "You've Come a Long Way, Baby—But Not as Far as You Thought," *Business Week*, 1 October 1984, p. 131.

5. John P. Kotter, *The General Managers* (New York: Free Press, 1982), p. 47.

6. Charlotte Decker Sutton and Kris K. Moore, "Executive Women—20 Years Later," *Harvard Business Review* 63 (September–October 1985): 66.

7. Ibid., p. 52.

8. Basia Hellwig, "The Breakthrough Generation: 73 Women Ready to Run Corporate America," *Working Woman* (April 1985): 148.

9. "The Ax Falls Increasingly on Top-Management Women," *Wall Street Journal*, 9 September 1986, p. 1.

10. Sutton and Moore, "Executive Women," p. 60.

11. Ibid.

12. Rosabeth Moss Kanter, "Mastering Change: The Skills We Need," in *Not as Far as You Think: The Realities of Working Women*, ed. Lynda L. Moore (Lexington, Mass.: D. C. Heath, Lexington Books, 1986), p. 185.

13. Aaron Bernstein, "Business Starts Tailoring Itself to Suit Working Women," *Business Week*, 6 October 1986, p. 51.

14. David Wessel, "The Last Angry Men," *Wall Street Journal*, 24 March 1986, p. 20D.

15. Irene Pave, "A Woman's Place Is at GE, Federal Express, P&G . . . ," *Business Week*, 23 June 1986, p. 75.

16. Edward W. Jones, Jr., "Black Managers: The Dream Deferred," *Harvard Business Review* 64 (May–June 1986): 93.

17. Jane Ciabattari, "The Biggest Mistake Top Managers Make," *Working Woman* (October 1986): 48.

18. Anne B. Fisher, "Businessmen Like to Hire by the Numbers," *Fortune*, 16 September 1985, p. 28.

Index

Accountability, 65, 107, 124
Achievement via
  conformance, 50, 52
Appearance. *See* Image
AT&T, 6

Bad bosses, 3, 35, 77, 83–84,
  103, 106
Bank of America, 6
Barriers to promotion, 4–5,
  13–14, 123–26, 139–54,
  157, 166
Bias. *See* Discrimination
Blacks, 11, 39, 69, 80, 166,
  167–68. *See also* Minority
  men
Borman, Frank, 19
Borman, Susan, 19
Business Week, 157, 166

Career management, 85–92,
  171
Catalyst, 49, 50

Center for Creative
  Leadership, 9, 50, 192–94
  Executive Women Project,
  8–10, 53, 177–80, 183–86,
  201–18
  Research Sponsor Program,
  7, 24, 43, 53, 58, 181–82
Chassler, Scy, 33
Chemical Bank, 6
Chief executives officers,
  women as. *See* Executive
  women, chief executive
  officers
Childcare aid, 166
Childlessness (as a choice),
  115–16
Children. *See* Parenting;
  Pregnancy
Childress, Georgia P., 39
Claiborne, Liz, 6
Coaching. *See* Help from
  above
Colleges and universities,
  prestigious, 129, 130, 156

Community work, 97, 130, 131, 171
Compensation for women. *See* Salaries for women
Conference Board, 166
Corporate culture, 36, 75, 92, 111, 158, 171
Cosell, Hilary, 14, 19
Courses. *See* Training programs
Culture. *See* Corporate culture

Day care centers. *See* Childcare aid
Derailment, 16, 18, 67, 75, 98, 136, 141, 172
  cases, 23, 34–36, 62, 114
  of women vs. men, 43–44, 68, 189
Derailment factors, 23, 36–43, 53, 62, 189
  in success cases, 41–42, 188
Discrimination, 19, 72, 86–87, 157, 164
  as a barrier, 140, 141, 153
Dress. *See* Image
DuPont, 168

EEO. *See* Equal Employment Opportunity legislation
Entrepreneurs, women as, 5, 141, 150–51, 173
Equal Employment Opportunity legislation, 26–27, 63, 68, 134, 135

and Reagan administration, 147, 158–59, 168
Evans, Jane, 20, 155
Executive women:
  chief executive officers, 6, 137, 140, 150, 155, 164–65
  compared with executive men, 48–54, 68–70, 85–89, 113, 152
  pressures on, 15–20, 69, 153, 165, 169, 170
  profile, 10–12, 177, 179–80
  vice presidents, 6, 35, 87, 89, 98, 111
  younger men's attitudes toward, 156, 160–61, 167
Executive Women Project. *See* Center for Creative Leadership, Executive Women Project

Failure. *See* Derailment
Family life, 10–11, 28–29, 63–64, 91, 103, 113–22, 151, 153, 166–67
  strains on, 4, 17, 18, 104–05, 106, 113, 118, 147–48, 161. *See also* Parenting
Feedback, 37, 41, 42, 76, 77–78, 83, 103–04, 105, 171–72
Femininity, 33, 47, 54, 55, 62–63
  as a tool or weapon, 4, 63, 78–79

"vive la différence"
    attitude, 48
Fitting in, 37, 75, 79, 81–82,
    111, 112
Forbes, 137
Fortune, 6, 150, 151, 155, 168

Gannett Company, 167
Garland, Howard, 136
General Electric (GE), 6
General management,
    definition of, 13–14, 124
Glass ceiling. *See* Barriers to
    promotion
Golden West Financial Corp.,
    6
Graham, Katharine, 6, 137
Graham, Philip, 137

Harlan, Anne, 18–19, 52, 64
Harvard Business Review, 158,
    159, 160, 161, 167–68
Hellwig, Basia, 29, 30, 125,
    159
Help from above, 77, 94–95,
    100–01, 126, 132–34, 147,
    162, 171
    as a success factor, 23, 24,
    25–27, 42. *See also*
    Feedback

Iacocca, Lee, 168
IBM, 6
Image, 12, 32–33, 40, 43, 44,
    61, 73–74

Indsco, 39
Intelligence, 32, 35, 42, 74, 77,
    99
Interpersonal skills. *See*
    People skills

Jones, Edward W., Jr., 167

Kanter, Rosabeth Moss, 16–
    17, 26, 38–39, 132, 166
Korn/Ferry International, 32
Kotter, John P., 158

Line positions, 11, 71, 90, 127,
    139, 168, 171
    change to, from staff
    positions, 3, 21, 22, 30,
    31, 58, 67, 87–88, 140,
    143–45
Loden, Marilyn, 49
Lombardo, Michael M., 7
Luck, 134–37, 172

Management Skills Profile,
    52, 195–200
Management style, 34–35, 47,
    49, 52, 62, 94
    different from boss's style,
    83, 97, 100, 105
Managers, women as. *See*
    Executive women
McCall, Morgan W., Jr., 7
Marriage. *See* Family life

"Masculine" traits (in women), 37, 54, 55–56, 61–63, 79. *See also* Toughness
Maternity leave, 166
MBAs, women with, 6, 62, 64, 97, 106
Mead Corporation, 167
Merck & Company, 167
Middle management, women in, 5, 20, 54, 156
Mentors. *See* Help from above
Milwid, Beth, 53
Minority men, 68, 69, 108–09, 166, 168. *See also* Blacks
Money. *See* Salaries for women

Nepotism. *See* Relatives (male) of company leaders
Networking, 15–16, 33, 78, 101, 171
New Yorker, 24

Parenting, 113, 116, 120–22, 140, 153, 173
Pay. *See* Salaries for women
People skills, 22, 29–30, 32, 33, 43, 44, 97, 109
Perception, 12, 23–24, 53, 70, 103, 171
Performance expectations for women, 44, 47–48, 53–67, 69–70, 146, 150, 169–70

Personal relationships, 17–18, 113, 114, 118–19, 122, 151. *See also* Family life
Personnel Decisions, Inc., 52, 195
Peter Principle, 39
Politics, 56, 83, 84, 98, 110–11
Pregnancy, 116–17, 119–20, 153, 166. *See also* Maternity leave
Presence. *See* Image
Price, Kenneth H., 136

Relatives (male) of company leaders, 68, 69
Reorganization, 135–36
Research Sponsor Program. *See* Center for Creative Leadership, Research Sponsor Program
Risk taking, 30–31, 42, 57–60, 93, 94–95

Salaries for women, 64, 82, 86–87, 125, 173
Sandler, Marion, 6
Savvy, 53
Savvy insiders, description of, 23, 177
Self-confidence, 92–98
Self-employment. *See* Entrepreneurs, women as
Seminars. *See* Training programs

Sex differences. *See* Derailment, of women vs. men; Executive women, compared with executive men; Success factors, for women vs. for men

Sex role stereotypes, 51–52, 53–56, 58, 69, 90, 145. *See also* Femininity; "Masculine" traits (in women)

Spence, Janet, 164

Sponsors. *See* Help from above

Staff positions, 11, 21, 27, 96, 102, 127, 142. *See also* Line positions, change to, from staff positions

Stereotypes, sex role. *See* Sex role stereotypes

Strober, Myra, 150

Success factors, 22–34, 53, 75, 83, 187
    for women vs. for men, 44–45, 53, 64, 68, 136, 190
    in derailment cases, 41–42, 187

Success, lessons for, 70, 74–98, 100–22, 210–11

Top managers, women as. *See* Executive women

Toughness, 48, 61–63, 106, 109, 112
    as a success factor, 24, 31–32, 44. *See also* "Masculine" traits (in women)

Trade groups, 131

Traditional sex roles. *See* Sex role stereotypes

Training programs, 96, 171

Trust, 30, 66–67, 81

United Way, 130–31

USA Today, 6

Von Glinow, Mary Ann, 5

Wachner, Linda, 6

Wall. *See* Barriers to promotion

Wall Street Journal, 6, 16, 68, 69, 151, 159, 167

Warnaco, 6

Washington Post, 137

Weiss, Carol, 18–19, 52, 64

Wood, Marion, 10, 11

Working Woman, 30, 32, 125, 156

ENNIS AND NANCY HAM LIBRARY
ROCHESTER COLLEGE
800 WEST AVON ROAD
ROCHESTER HILLS, MI 48307